THE
freethinker's
PRAYER
BOOK

THE
freethinker's
PRAYER
BOOK

AND SOME WORDS TO LIVE BY

KHUSHWANT SINGH

ALEPH

ALEPH

ALEPH BOOK COMPANY
An independent publishing firm
promoted by *Rupa Publications India*

First published in India in 2012 by
Aleph Book Company
7/16 Ansari Road, Daryaganj
New Delhi 110002

ISBN: 9788192328041

1 3 5 7 9 10 8 6 4 2

Typeset in 11 pts Goudy Old Style by SÜRYA, New Delhi

Printed and bound in India by
Replika Press Pvt. Ltd.
310–311 EPIP Kundli,
Haryana 131028

· Contents ·

· Introduction ·

By the time this book is published, I will be ninety-seven. I am a very old man. And there is one eternal truth I can tell you right away: Old age is not pleasant; it buggers up your life. I am not yet senile, but my memory, of which I was very proud, is failing. Though I can still read, my hands shake so much that it is difficult to write anything legible. I have been spared the indignity of shitting in bed pans and having nurses wipe my bottom, but I often need assistance to get to the toilet. I am on more pills than I can count. In short, my body is giving up. It is time to say alvida and depart. I am reminded of these lines by John Keats:

Now more than ever seems it rich to die,
To cease upon the midnight with no pain . . .

In the *Mahabharata* it is written, 'Man grows old, but not desire.' That great show-off, Oscar Wilde, said it more dramatically: 'The tragedy of old age is not that one is old, but that one is young.' They are both right. This is another reason why advanced age is a nuisance. The heart desires all the things you did in your youth, but time slowly robs you of the means to get them.

But I should not complain. I have lived a reasonably contented life, and it will be easy to go. Sometimes, however, I wish I knew where to. I am not a man of faith. Since I do not believe in paradise or the possibility of rebirth, I have no idea where I will be after I die. It is like staring into an endless dark void. Paul Valery put it very well: 'Death speaks to us in a very deep voice but has nothing to say.'

For many years I dreaded death. To cure myself of the phobia, I would go to the cremation ground at Delhi's Nigambodh Ghat and watch corpses burn to ashes and bone. It was cathartic. It cleansed me of petty vanities and anxieties and I returned home at peace with myself. But it did not help me overcome my fear. Now, I am no longer afraid of dying—in fact, the end will be welcome, as long as it is swift and painless. I have made my peace with the great void. But I still don't know where I will be after I breathe my last.

People who have religion seem to derive comfort from the belief that they will meet their Maker after they die, or that they will be reborn in some form. The more self-righteous among them are convinced that they will ascend straight to heaven. As an agnostic, I have no such comfort.

So be it. I have no regrets.

I was born into an orthodox Sikh family in Hadali (now in Pakistan), and as a child I liked the rituals of my faith. I was a good boy, my grandmother's favourite, because I could recite my morning and evening prayers by rote and sing a shabad or two in the village gurdwara. I barely understood the words, but that did not seem to matter because few of my elders understood or made any attempt to understand what they recited every day. By the time I was fifteen or sixteen, I had begun to question ritual and religious dogma. At Delhi's newly opened Modern School, I was learning how science, technology and the liberal arts were transforming the western world. There was nothing scientific or liberal about religion as I saw it practised around me. But I did not want to invite trouble at home and kept my doubts to myself. At the age of seventeen, I underwent the ceremony of sipping amrit (holy water) and became a member of the Khalsa Panth, the fraternity of the pure.

In college, my conviction that religion was irrational and encouraged superstition and ignorance grew stronger. I also saw how it generated more prejudice and hatred than love and friendship. In Sikhism, for instance, the abhorrent practice of untouchability is forbidden, but I saw almost all my elders discriminate against converts from the 'low' castes. I also found it ironic that the followers of Guru Nanak, the founder of the Sikh faith who proclaimed God to be nirankaar (formless) and forbade the worship of idols, treated the Guru Granth Sahib, the compilation of Nanak's and other Gurus' writings, as an idol worthy of worship. They draped it in silk and brocade, roused it in the morning (prakash) and put it to rest in the evenings (santokh). It wasn't among the Sikhs alone that I noticed rituals which made a travesty of their faith—Hindus, Muslims and Christians were all alike in this. I gradually gave up on organized religion. Yet, I continued to retain the outward emblems of the Khalsa because it gave me a sense of belonging and social security, as it does to this day.

It also took me some time to free myself of the habit of prayer. I gave it up off and on, but returned to it when in physical pain or fear or under emotional stress. When my relations with my wife once came to breaking point and she told me that she meant to leave me, I spent the whole night at Gurdwara Bangla Sahib praying for strength to face the crisis. Many a time in Tokyo, when I got up at three in the morning to work on the translations of the hymns of Guru Nanak, I felt the hand of the Guru on my shoulder. Though I knew it was make-believe, I found it very comforting.

Eventually, I lost the habit of prayer as well. However, my interest in the Sikh faith and scriptures remained. I also became interested in the sacred texts of other major religions: Christianity, Hinduism, Islam, Judaism, Jainism, Buddhism, Zoroastrianism and the Bahái faith. I studied the world's religions and met gurus, babas and matas with the curiosity of a dispassionate observer. I even taught comparative religion for a period in the 1960s, at the universities of Princeton and Hawaii. I did this as a complete agnostic, because by my thirties I had stopped believing that there was a God. Nothing since has convinced me otherwise.

The most endearing attempt to make a believer of me was made by a little girl some twenty-five years ago. I had written an article in *The Indian Express* spelling out my views on God and religion. Soon after, I received a letter from Supriya, the twelve-year-old daughter of the then editor of the paper, Rajmohan Gandhi. 'Dear Uncle,' she wrote, 'I read your article in Daddy's paper. So you don't believe in God? You are wrong! Let me tell you, God exists. He visits our garden every day. He talks to my Mummy and my Daddy. He also talks to me and my little brother. So there!' I was charmed and wrote back: 'Dear Supriya, I am glad to hear that God visits your garden every day. And that He talks to your Mummy, Daddy, you and your brother. But He does not talk to me. Please send me His telephone number.' Supriya did not reply. Three years later I met her parents in Delhi. They told me ruefully, 'Supriya no longer believes in God.' I was delighted that I had won a convert in the great-grandchild of two great believers in God, Mahatma Gandhi and C. Rajagopalachari.

Many people have argued with me about the existence of God, trying to prove me wrong. I have always responded with simple logic: there is not a shred of credible evidence to support what they say. Despite the occasional claims by mystics, the truth is that no one has seen God. No one has been able to define God besides investing him with innumerable fantastic attributes: He is the creator, preserver and destroyer; benevolent and helpful; wrathful as well as just. He is everything and he is also, as the Upanishads say, *neti, neti*—not this, not this. The truth is that no one has a clue. It is more honest to admit that we don't know, rather than accept fairy tales about God having created the world in six days or in the blink of an eye.

The Voltarian argument that if there is a watch there must then be a watchmaker has never made sense to me. I have met a few watchmakers, I have never met God. If God created the universe, who created God? If an all-powerful, all-seeing God does exist, why is there injustice and suffering in the world? Even those who believe in God have little justification for describing Him as omnipotent and just. Whatever evidence we have is to the contrary. Some children are born with severe physical and mental disabilities; God-fearing parents who never harmed anyone in their lives are punished by the loss of their innocent children; the gentlest people suffer terribly while thieves and murderers prosper. I cannot accept a God who is selective in granting his grace, or who is blind. And a 'Mighty Avenger' who must be constantly appeased is no God at all.

Even as a concept, God fails. Belief in God has little bearing on making a person good or bad. In our country alone, for every Mother Teresa and Baba Amte, there are thousands who have killed and raped in the name of their gods, as was done during Partition on both sides of the border, in Delhi in 1984 and in Gujarat in 2002. The masterminds of the 1984 and 2002 pogroms are ministers and party leaders. Neither the law nor God has made them pay for their crimes.

Rejecting the idea of God and giving up on the basics of religion was not easy. It required searching within myself and questioning beliefs on which I had been nurtured. And once I had done it, how would I fill the vacuum? How could one explain the universe, life on earth and the laws of nature? Reason and logic helped me demolish much that I had been brought up on, but they did not give me all the answers I was looking for. So began the quest for a personal religion. Iqbal echoed my sentiments:

Dhoondta phirta hoon main, ai Iqbal, apney aap ko
Aap hi goya musaafir, aap hi manzil hoon main.

(O Iqbal, I go about everywhere looking for myself
As if I was the wayfarer as well as the destination.)

Over some years, I came up with a religion of my own. It had very simple rules: ahimsa—non-violence—above all; work as worship; honesty (even about one's dishonesties); helping people in need; silent charity; and respecting and preserving the natural world. I may have failed to live by these rules sometimes, but I have tried to do so to the best of my ability.

My role models have never been the pious who contemplate God and the Universe in the seclusion of caves or by the banks of holy rivers. Rather, they are people who work among the poor and the handicapped. Mother Teresa, Bhagat Puran Singh, Ela Bhatt and Baba Amte are worth more than a hundred Shankaracharyas, Chinmayanandas and other godmen put together. They are our true saints, not those who merely pray and meditate or give long sermons to the gullible. I do not dismiss prayer altogether—one does not have to believe in God to concede that prayer has power. But all that it does is comfort the person saying the prayer. To change the world, you need to get out of your temples and do some useful work. I am more than ready to respect any baba, sant or maulvi if he joins the man breaking stones to build a road.

All my life I have also believed that since we have only one life to live, it is our duty to live well and be happy. Renunciation does not impress me. It is self-righteous and anti-life—as Rumi said, 'People who renounce desire turn suddenly into hypocrites.' For all its imperfections, life is a great gift, and I have tried to get as much out of it as I could. I have feasted my eyes and senses on all that is beautiful in the world: its mountains and lakes, seashores and deserts; the break of the monsoon and the scent of wet earth; good food from all parts of the world, vintage wines and the finest Scotch whiskey; western classical music and shabad-kirtan; the fragrance of flowers and herbs and the shade of mighty trees; birdsong at the break of dawn; classic literature; and beautiful, spirited women, preferably with the gift of gossip. To quote the English poet and journalist, Arthur St. John Adcock:

> *Come, let us go a-roaming!*
> *The world is all our own,*
> *And half its paths are still untrod,*
> *And half its joys unknown.*

I would sum up my faith in a time-worn cliché: a good life is the only religion. A life of giving happiness and also finding it for oneself. There are better words to say it, for which I turn to the nineteenth-century American political leader and orator Robert G. Ingersoll: 'Happiness is the only good; the place to be happy is here; the time to be happy is now; the way to be happy is to help others.' And to Bertrand Russell, who, having rejected religion, came up with his own rules for life: 'I believe in using words, not fists. I believe in honesty. I believe in a good time. I believe in good food. I believe in sex.'

My personal religion set me free long ago. I am no respecter of any single faith in its totality. I pick and choose as I please. All religions were creatures of their times and evolved to meet prevailing social and economic needs. To describe them as eternal truths for all time to come is sheer bunkum. But alongside all that is irrational, absurd and dangerous in every religion, there is also some good sense and nobility. It is the same with prophets and saints, as it is with philosophers, scientists and political leaders.

Once you have decided not to bow to any gods, and if you have a good bullshit detector, it is possible to separate the sublime from the ridiculous and derive inspiration from the words of prophets and poets, gurus and rogues, grave men and clowns. There is a lot to be learned from both the sacred and the profane. I have done that nearly all my life and put down in my notebooks hundreds of lines from different sources that appealed to me. Sometimes I ask the more interesting people who come to visit me to write their favourite aphorisms and quotes in a diary I keep especially for this purpose. The best of these have been collected in the pages that follow. They are not all prayers; there are also precepts, advice, snatches of song and verse, and some words to live by. I offer them to you as life codes from an ancient and unrepentant agnostic. Read them with an open mind and an open heart.

· A Note on the Book ·

Many scriptures, like the Buddhist, Jain and Zoroastrian texts, the Guru Granth Sahib, the Bible and the Tao Teh Ching, contain the teachings of the founders or best-known prophets of the respective religions. Hence, excerpts from some scriptures appear in two sections, 'The Books and Other Holy Texts' and 'Prophets, Mystics and Saints'.

Similarly, a few poets and philosophers who are fellow agnostics or mavericks I admire, appear in two sections—'Poets, Philosophers and Other Wordsmiths' and 'One Last Miscellany'.

It is the tradition to give the exact section and lines when quoting from some of the major scriptures or epics. This, however, is not possible for every text. For reasons of consistency, therefore, only the main scripture or book—and in some cases the section—has been mentioned as the source.

Wherever a translation has not been attributed, it is either my own, or adapted from translations in the public domain. The only exceptions are translations of verses by the Kashmiri saint Hazrat Nuruddin Nurani, or Nund Rishi, on pages 68 and 87. I have been unable to locate the book from which I copied these translations several years ago.

I would like to thank all the people who have contributed

to this selection, either by translating work especially for it or by granting permission to use their published translations. A detailed page of acknowledgments is included at the end of the book.

THE BOOKS
and
OTHER HOLY
TEXTS

.....

Most people believe the texts of their faith alone contain the greatest truths. You cannot argue with them. I have spent a lifetime reading the sacred books of different religions, and I'm surprised by the passions they arouse. If people bothered to get at the exact meaning of the prayers they chant, they would stop thinking of themselves as the chosen ones. At its heart, every scripture says the same thing. There would be much less prejudice in the world if people tried to read as much as possible from the different scriptures and knew something about each other's faiths.

But our holy books are not always humane and full of wisdom. When religions get prescriptive, they do more harm than good. They tell us what to eat and drink, how to cook, how to bathe, what to wear, whom to love and bed, how to procreate and how to dispose of our dead. We follow these rules blindly, which is the cause of great trouble and stupidity in the world. But the biggest failure of every major religion is the notion of hell and perdition. Is it not strange that the same books that tell us to love our neighbours and forgive our enemies also declare that unbelievers and doubters will burn in hell?

Indeed, I could produce a bigger collection than this one if I sat down to catalogue all that I find intolerant, violent and nonsensical in the world's religions. But I have also found enough that is moving and worthy of admiration. These are the words I have included in this section.

In my selection I have also been guided by literary quality. Most religious prose and poetry is repetitive and banal. But patient reading reveals passages of genuine literary merit. The Guru Granth Sahib, for instance, contains verse that uses images from nature to exquisite effect. The Bible has beautiful lines of verse, written in utterly simple language shorn of literary conceits. Their message goes straight to the readers' hearts and stays there.

Likewise, the hymns in the Upanishads and the Vedas have some of the most majestic images and ideas found in any literature. And verses from the Quran have the power to move people to tears. Numerous passages can be read and re-read for their literary excellence and emotive quality—Sura Rehman (The Merciful), Sura Nissa (The Heights), Sura Al Dhariyat (The Winds) and many others.

Since I am not obliged to hold any scripture as sacrosanct, I think I have been able to cull the valuable and memorable from each holy book, ignoring a lot that is of indifferent literary quality, illogical or contrary to a humane and liberal world view.

It seems appropriate to my agnostic mind to start this prayer book with the most audacious challenge ever posed to believers. Here are the concluding lines of the Nasadiya Sukta, the Creation Hymn, from the **Rig Veda**, arguably the world's most ancient sacred text. This version is adapted from translations by Wendy Doniger and A.L. Basham:

> Who knows, then, where everything arose?
> Who can say how Creation happened?
> The gods themselves came after Creation.
>
> Then He, whether He created all that is or whether
> He did not;
> He, who looks upon everything from the highest heaven—
> He alone knows. Or maybe He too does not.

If a man say, I love God, and hateth his brother, he is a liar:
For he that loveth not his brother whom he hath seen,
cannot love God whom he hath not seen.

~ The Bible

O people! We created you from the same male and female
[but] made you into [separate] nations and tribes so that
you may know and honour each other, and in the eyes of
God the most honourable among you is the most righteous.
For God is all-knowing.

~ The Quran

There is One God.
He is the Supreme Truth.
He, the Creator,
Is without fear and without hate.
He, the Omnipresent,
Pervades the universe.

~ Opening lines of the *Guru Granth Sahib*

Let us live happily, then, not hating those who hate us.
Among men who hate us, let us dwell free from hatred.

~ The Dhammapada

All the Arihants [the enlightened ones] of all times
proclaim this:
Do not injure, abuse, oppress, enslave, insult, torment,
torture or kill any living being.
That which you destroy or think of destroying
is (like) yourself.
That which you subjugate or think of subjugating
is (like) yourself.
That which you kill or think of killing
is (like) yourself.

~ The Akaranga Sutra,
one of the oldest religious texts of the Jains

We revere Good Thoughts, Good Words, Good Deeds
done and to be done, now and henceforth.
And we, therefore, praise and invoke
all that is Good.

~ The Avesta

He said to them: 'What should a man seek for himself?'

Rabbi Eliezer said, 'A good eye.'
Rabbi Yehoshua said, 'A good friend.'
Rabbi Yose said, 'A good neighbour.'
Rabbi Shimon said, 'The ability to see the consequences.'
Rabbi Elazar said, 'A good heart.'

And he said to them: 'I prefer the words of Rabbi Elazar,
because his words include the words of all the rest.'

~ 'Ethics of the Fathers', The Talmud

Blessed are the merciful:
for they shall obtain mercy.
Blessed are the pure in heart:
for they shall see God.
Blessed are the peacemakers:
for they shall be called the children of God.

~ The Bible

Give birth to and nourish all things,
without desiring to possess them.
Give of yourself,
without expecting something in return.
Assist people,
but do not attempt to control them.
This is how you realize the deep virtue of the Universe.

~ Tao Teh Ching
{translation by Hua-Ching Ni}

O you beloved of the Lord! Commit not that which defiles
the limpid stream of love or destroys the sweet fragrance of
friendship. By the righteousness of the Lord!
You were created to show love one to another
and not perversity and rancour.
Take pride not in love for yourselves but in love for your
fellow creatures. Glory not in love for your country, but in
love for all mankind . . .
Set your reliance on the army of justice,
put on the armour of wisdom, let your adorning
be forgiveness and mercy.

~ Tablet of Wisdom, Bahá'u'lláh

There are five prayers,
Each with a time and name of its own.
First, truthfulness.
Second, to take only what is your due.
Third, goodwill towards all.
Fourth, pure intentions;
And praise of God, the fifth.
~ *The Guru Granth Sahib*

Lead us from untruth to Truth,
Lead us from darkness to Light,
Lead us from death to Eternity.
[Let there be] Peace. Peace. Peace.
~ *Brihadaranyaka Upanishad*

The glory of the man of wisdom is also the glory of
the man of good action.
That man sees the Truth, who sees that thought
and action are one.
~ *The Bhagavad Gita*

Be a lamp unto yourself.
Be a refuge to yourself.
Hold fast to the Truth as a lamp.
Hold fast to the Truth as a refuge.
Look not for refuge outside yourself.

~ *Maha Parinibbana Sutta,*
based on the last days of the Buddha

O you who believe! Stand out firmly for justice, as
witnesses to God, even against yourselves, or your
parents, or your kin, and whether it be against rich or
poor, for God can best protect both.
Follow not the cravings of your hearts, lest you swerve,
and if you distort justice or decline to do justice, truly
God is well acquainted with all that you do.

~ *The Quran*
{translation by Abdullah Yusuf Ali}

Do not mock anyone.
Do not be over-zealous in punishing others.
Do not strike others.
Do not tell a lie to anyone.
Do not deceive anyone lest you come to grief thereby.
Do not destroy your own soul through anger or vengeance.

~ *Counsels of Adarbad Mahraspandan,*
a sacred text of the Zoroastrians

Conquer the untruthful man with truthfulness;
Subdue the angry man with gentleness;
Overcome the evil man with goodness.

~ *The Mahabharata*

Overcome anger with kindness,
And evil with good.
Overcome meanness with a gift,
And a liar with truth.

~ *The Dhammapada*

The true yogi meditates, realizing
. . . I am a stranger to this world,
there is no one with me!
Just as the spume and the waves
are born of the ocean then melt back into it,
So the world is born of me and melts back into me.

~ *Yoga Darshana Upanishad*
{translation by Jean Varenne and Derek Coltman}

Learn to let go.
~ *Isha Upanishad*

The Sikh Guru Arjun Dev, in **Shabad Hazare**, *had this advice for those who want to practise asceticism:*

Let your own house be the forest,
Your heart the anchorite.
Eat little, sleep little,
Learn to love, be merciful, and forbear.
Be mild, be patient,
Have no lust, nor wrath,
Greed, nor obstinacy.

Do not turn your face away from your fellow men,
And do not walk in insolence upon the earth.
For God does not favour the arrogant.

~ *The Quran*
{translation by Zia Hashmi}

He whose mind is free from anxiety in the face of suffering,
who is indifferent to pleasure as to pain,
who is beyond passion, fear, anger and hate—
he alone is the most excellent sage.

~ *The Bhagavad Gita*

Not about the perversities of others,
not about their sins of commission
nor their sins of omission,
but about his own misdeeds and negligences alone
should a sage be worried.

~ *The Dhammapada*
{translation by Paul Carus}

Sweet blow the winds.
Sweet flow the rivers.
May the herbs be sweet to us.
May the night and days bring happiness.
May the dust of the Earth yield us happiness.
May Heaven, our Father, send us happiness.
May the trees gladden us with fruit.
May the Sun bestow joy on us.
May every direction bring us happiness.

~ *The Rig Veda*
{translation by Renuka Narayanan}

And they shall beat their swords into plowshares,
and their spears into pruning hooks:
nation shall not lift up a sword against nation,
neither shall they learn war any more.

~ *The Bible*

A good soldier is not violent.
A good fighter is not angry.

~ *Tao Teh Ching*

Feeble or strong, short or tall,
small or large, seen or unseen;
near-dwelling or distant,
born and present in this world or yet to be born:
May all beings, without exception,
Be happy minded.

~ *Karaniya Metta Sutta*

Unto heaven be peace, unto the sky be peace,
Unto the earth, water, herbs, plants and trees be peace.
Unto the gods be peace, unto the Creator be peace,
Unto everyone be peace, and peace unto me.

~ *The Yajur Veda*
{translation by Renuka Narayanan}

Indeed, Ahura Mazda, the Wise God,
knows the people of righteousness:
They who serve the living world in which we all live.
And we, on our part, venerate all such men and women.

~ *The Zoroastrian Gathas*

Who is honoured?
He who honours mankind.
~ *'Ethics of the Fathers', The Talmud*

And thou shalt love the Lord thy God with all thy heart,
and with all thy soul, and with all thy mind, and with all
thy strength: this is the first commandment.
And the second is like, namely this,
Thou shalt love thy neighbour as thyself.
There is none other commandment greater than these.
~ *The Bible*

*The remarkable concept of Vasudhaivakutumbakam (the world is
our family) appears in this shloka from the* **Maha Upanishad**:

Only the small of heart think:
'These are my people, and those strangers.'
For the magnanimous sage,
All the world is family.

In making a gift we overcome greed, which is a
form of himsa (violence). Hence gifts made to those
in need amount to a renunciation of himsa
(and observance of ahimsa).

~ *Purusharthasiddhi-upaya,*
a Jain sacred text

Charity given without expectation of anything in return,
At the appropriate and auspicious time and place,
And given as a duty to those deserving—
Such charity is true goodness.

~ *The Bhagavad Gita*

A kind word followed by magnanimity is better than
charity followed by rudeness . . .
O believers, nullify not your alms-giving by
demanding gratitude or causing offence, like one
who spends his wealth in order to flaunt it before people
and believes neither in God nor in the Last Day.

~ *The Quran*
{translation by Tarif Khalidi}

Though I speak with the tongues of men and of angels,
and have not charity, I am become as sounding brass,
or a tinkling cymbal.
And though I have the gift of prophecy,
and understand all mysteries, and all knowledge;
and though I have all faith, so that I could remove
mountains, and have not charity, I am nothing.
And though I bestow all my goods to feed the poor,
and though I give my body to be burned,
and have not charity,
it profiteth me nothing.
~ *The Bible*

As a team of oxen are we driven
By the ploughman, our Teacher.
By the furrows made are thus writ
Our actions—on earth, our paper.
The sweat of labour is as beads
Falling, by the ploughman as seeds sown:
We reap according to our measure,
Some for ourselves to keep, some to others give.
O Nanak, this is the way to truly live.
~ *The Guru Granth Sahib*

Command those who are rich in this present world not to
be arrogant nor to put their hope in wealth, which is so
uncertain, but to put their hope in God, who richly
provides us with everything for our enjoyment.
Command them to do good, to be rich in good deeds,
and to be generous and willing to share.

~ The Bible

The deva said:
What is the greatest gain?
What is the greatest loss?
Which armour is invulnerable?
What is the best weapon?
The Blessed One replied:
The greatest gain is to give to others;
The greatest loss is to greedily receive without gratitude;
An invulnerable armour is patience;
The best weapon is wisdom.

~ The Gospel of the Buddha
{compiled from Buddhist texts and translated by Paul Carus}

Non-violence in thought, word and deed.
To seek and speak the truth.
To behave honestly and never to take anything
by force or theft.
To practise restraint and chastity in thought,
word and deed.
To practice non-acquisitiveness.

~ The five vratas (vows) in the Jain code of conduct

You will never come to piety
unless you spend of things you love;
and whatever you spend is known to God.

~ The Quran
{translation by Ahmed Ali}

The dharma one achieves by doing no violence to any
being, greater than that there is no dharma. Who causes in
others neither disquiet nor agitation, he becomes free
himself from fear.

~ The Mahabharata
{translation by Chaturvedi Badrinath}

People of the Book
do not go to excess
in your religion.
~ *The Quran*
{translation by Thomas Cleary}

Religion is not his who too much fasts
Or too much feasts, nor his who sleeps away
An idle mind; nor his who wears to waste
His strength in vigils. Nay, Arjuna! I call
That the true piety which most removes
Earth-aches and ills, where one is moderate
In eating and in resting, and in sport;
Measured in wish and act; sleeping betimes,
Waking betimes for duty.
~ *The Bhagavad Gita*
{translation by Edwin Arnold}

What use is bending or bowing of head
When you bow not the heart?
~ *The Guru Granth Sahib*

[The ignorant] seek comfort in mighty words;
Clever talking will not bring salvation.

~ *Uttaradhyayana,*
a text of the Jain canon

What seek you in pilgrimage to sacred rivers?
The priceless jewel is within your breast.
The learned Pundit reads much, declaims much
But knows not the treasure within himself.

~ *The Guru Granth Sahib*

There shall be no compulsion in the matter of faith.
Distinct is the way of guidance now from error.
He who turns from the forces of evil
and believes in God, will surely hold fast
to a handle that is strong and unbreakable,
for God hears all and knows everything.

~ *The Quran*

By self alone is evil done,
By self is one disgraced;
By self is evil left undone,
By self alone is one purified;
Purity and impurity belong to self:
No one can purify another.

~ *The Dhammapada*
{translation by A.J. Edmunds}

The knot of the heart is cut away,
Doubts vanish and struggles cease,
When That, the Truth, is seen.

~ *The Mundaka Upanishad*
{translation by Renuka Narayanan}

Not by refraining from action does man attain freedom
from [the consequences of] action. Not through mere
renunciation does he attain supreme perfection.

~ *The Bhagavad Gita*

Herein is our love made perfect, that we may have
boldness in the day of judgement: because as he is, so are
we in this world. There is no fear in love;
but perfect love casteth out fear: because fear hath torment.
He that feareth is not made perfect in love.

~ The Bible

In the name of Allah, most benevolent, ever-merciful.
Say: 'O you unbelievers,
I do not worship what you worship
Nor do you worship who I worship
Nor will I worship who you worship
Nor will you worship who I worship.
To you your way, to me my way.'

~ The Quran
{translation by Ahmed Ali}

Whoever does not love does not know God,
for God is love.

~ The Bible

Salutations to the God in the fire.
Salutations to the God in the earth.
Salutations to the God in the plants.
Salutations to the God in speech.
Salutations to the Lord of speech.
I offer my salutations to the Supreme Being,
the all-pervading Spirit.

~ *Taittiriya Upanishad*

O Ahura, rise within me,
grant me steadfastness of purpose.

~ *The Atash Nyaish prayer, the Zoroastrian Gathas*

Had He willed they would not have been idolaters.
We have not appointed you their guardian,
Nor are you their pleader.
Do not revile those who invoke
Others apart from God, lest they begin
To revile God out of malice and ignorance.

~ The Quran
{translation by Ahmed Ali}

He that is here in the human person,
and He that is there in the sun, are one.
He who knows thus attains, after desisting from this world,
this self made of food,
attains this self made of vital force,
attains this self made of mind,
attains this self made of intelligence,
attains this self made of bliss.

~ Taittiriya Upanishad
{translation by Swami Gambhirananda}

The prayer of Moses, which can apply to all of us, who hope for our words to communicate exactly what we mean:

My Lord! Open up for me my heart.
And ease for me my task.
And untie the knot of my tongue.
That they may understand my speech.
~ *The Quran*

For if the trumpet give an uncertain sound,
who shall prepare himself to the battle? So likewise ye,
except ye utter by the tongue words easy to be understood,
how shall it be known what is spoken?
For ye shall speak into the air.
~ *The Bible*

When you feel an urgent desire to do or say [something],
ask politely and say a prayer.
For no one ever broke his back by saying his prayers
or got foul breath by asking politely.
~ *Counsels of Adarbad Mahraspandan*

*Here is good advice on the 'middle path', central to the teachings of
the Buddhist masters:*

He who is skilled in doing good and
Who wishes to attain that state of calm [Nirvana]
should act thus:
He should be able, upright, perfectly upright,
Obedient, gentle and humble;
Contented, easily looked after (i.e., not a burden to others),
With few duties, simple in livelihood,
Controlled in senses, discreet, not impudent;
Not greedily attached to families.

~ *Karaniya Metta Sutta*
{translation by Sri Dhammananda}

To see without eyes,
Without ears, hear,
To walk without feet,
Without hands, work,
To speak without a tongue—
Thus living, yet detached from life.

~ *The Guru Granth Sahib*

Your dharma is to do your work [dispassionately]
Without any thought of the fruits of your effort.
Forsake all hope of reward and benefit.
~ *The Bhagavad Gita*

The Tathagata teaches a complete surrender of self,
but he does not teach a surrender of anything
to those powers that are evil, be they men or gods or
the elements of nature.
Struggle must be, for all life is a struggle of some kind.
But he that struggles should look to it
lest he struggle in the interest of self against truth
and righteousness.
~ *The Gospel of the Buddha*

Only he is human who does not let an act of kindness
go in vain.
The good that the other did to one should be repaid
by doing good to the other in even greater measure.
~ *The Mahabharata*
{translation by Chaturvedi Badrinath}

Three pages of sound commandments for practical living:

When you are greeted, return [the favour]
with a warmer greeting.
~ *The Quran*

We should blunt our sharp points, and unravel
the complication of things;
we should temper our brightness, and bring ourselves
into agreement with the obscurity of others.
~ *Tao Teh Ching*

Do not say anything that has a double meaning.
~ *Counsels of Adarbad Mahraspandan*

He that gives should never remember, he that receives
should never forget.
~ *The Talmud*

Arise! Watch. Remember and forget not.
~ *The Dhammapada*

A man has no better thing under the sun, than to eat,
and to drink, and to be merry: for that shall abide
with him in his labour all the days of his life,
which God gives him under the sun.

~ *The Bible*

Austerities done for honour, praise or reward are impure.

~ *The Bhagavad Gita*

Don't be proud if you gain.
Nor be sorry if you lose.

~ *The Akaranga Sutra*

In the realm of action, effort is supreme,
nothing else prevails.

~ *The Guru Granth Sahib*

Eliminate all mental obscurity, and instead embrace
crystal clarity.

~ *Lao Tzu's Hua Hu Ching*
{translation by Hua-Ching Ni}

One's speech should be marked with affection and
tenderness towards all human beings, and with
pleasantness to the ears.
To cause anguish to others by hurting and
wounding words are low acts.

~ *The Mahabharata*
{translation by Chaturvedi Badrinath}

O children of Adam,
Adorn yourselves,
And eat well and drink well,
But do not be extravagant:
For God does not favour
The immoderate and the wasteful.

~ *The Quran*

And the most delightful commandment of all:

So far as you possibly can, do not bore your fellow men.

~ *Counsels of Adarbad Mahraspandan*

Home have I left, for I have left my world!
Child have I left, and all my cherished herds!
Lust have I left, and ill-will, too, is gone,
And Ignorance have I put far from me;
Craving and root of craving overpowered,
Cool am I now, knowing Nibbana's [Nirvana's] peace.

~ *from* The Therigatha, or Verses of the Elder Nuns
{translation by C.A.F. Rhys Davids}

Religion lieth not in the patched coat the Yogi wears,
Not in the staff he bears,
Nor in the ashes on his body.
Religion lieth not in rings in the ears,
Not in a shaven head,
Nor in the blowing of the conch shell.
If thou must the path of true religion see
Amongst the world's impurities, be of impurities free.

~ *The Guru Granth Sahib*

Let no one deceive another nor despise any
Person whatsoever in any place.
In anger or ill-will,
Let him not wish any harm to another.

~ *Karaniya Metta Sutta*
{translation by Sri Dhammananda}

No action debases the man of integrity who is master of
his life and whose soul is one with the soul of all.
~ *The Bhagavad Gita*

They earn swiftly the grace and forgiveness of God—
And the Garden [of paradise] made for the righteous—
Who spend [in charity] in good times and bad,
Who are not ruled by anger and pardon all men.
~ *The Quran*

Victory breeds anger
For the vanquished is ever in pain.
The man of peace knows happiness
For he is beyond victory and defeat.
There is no fire like passion,
No evil luck like hate,
No happiness higher than peace.
~ *The Dhammapada*

I ask forgiveness of all living beings,
May all living beings grant me forgiveness.
My friendship is with all living beings,
My heart is completely free of enmity.

~ *Khamemi Savve Jiva,*
a Jain prayer

[God] has no name, no dwelling place, no caste;
He is the Primal being, Gracious and Benign . . .
He is of no nation and wears no distinguishing garb;
He has no outer likeness; He is free from desire.
To the east or the west
Look where you may,
He pervades and prevails
As love and affection.

~ *The Dasam Granth of Guru Gobind Singh*

Now the end of the commandment is love, out of a pure
heart, and a good conscience and a faith unfeigned.

~ *The Bible*

May everyone be happy,
May everyone be free of illness,
May everyone have good fortune,
May everyone be free of suffering.

~ *Brihadaranyaka Upanishad*
{translation by Renuka Narayanan}

The Almighty troubleth me.

~ *The Bible*

PROPHETS,
MYSTICS
and
SAINTS

.....

There are people who may be open-minded about the existence of God. But few will tolerate anyone questioning the divinity of the founder of their religion. The Prophet is more revered than God.

One can see why this is the case. Gods are remote, Prophets are less so. They were born human; they ate, broke wind, defecated; they fell sick and died. While we may deny in outrage that our Prophets were tainted by bodily needs and functions or that they actually died, it cannot be denied that we claim to know everything about them because they were, like us, human beings. Which cannot be the case with God, hence the greater attachment to our Prophets.

The founders and leading saints of all religions were indeed remarkable and charismatic people who influenced millions and changed the course of history. This does not, however, justify our investing them with magical powers and putting them above mere reference and discussion, leave alone critical assessment. *'Ba Khuda diwana basho/Ba Mohammed hoshiar'* (Say anything you like about Allah, but beware of what you say about Mohammed) applies not just to followers of Islam but to the religious-minded of all communities.

The greater tribute to Prophets and saints would be to give them respect as important thinkers and historical personages, make an objective assessment of their life and ideas and adopt the best of what they preached. By doing this, we will also be able to better appreciate the wisdom and beauty of their words. Worshipping them and taking everything they uttered to be the immutable word of God is neither fair to them nor to us.

In this section you will find no contemporary godmen or godwomen. I have even less time for cults than I have for organized religion. But there is one living person who is here—The Dalai Lama, because he is a wise and gentle man, and the religious leader of the remarkable Tibetan people; and there are two people from our very recent history: Mahatma Gandhi and Mother Teresa.

I admire Bapu Gandhi more than any other human being. No one was more honest, and no one did more to spread the message of ahimsa (non-violence). His life was his message. He had his foibles and he could be very strange. He went to bizarre lengths in his experiments with celibacy, sleeping naked next to young girls to test himself. But he never lied even about such unusual behaviour. He bared himself; he had no fear of failure or criticism. And he could forgive. He never committed an act of deliberate violence in word or deed.

After Bapu, Mother Teresa is the person I admire most. She dedicated her entire life to the care of the sick and the dying. I asked her once if she had never found it repellant to hold people with diseases that covered their bodies with sores, or to tend to very sick people lying on Calcutta's roads in filth and excrement. She replied, 'I see Jesus in every human being. I say to myself, This is hungry Jesus. This one has gangrene, dysentery or cholera. I mush wash him and tend to him.' If her faith could give her such compassion, who was I to question it?

After our first meeting, I put her on the cover of *The Illustrated Weekly of India* and wrote about her for *The New York Times*. She sent me a note of thanks, which is among my most prized possessions and hangs in a silver frame in my house in Kasauli. The note ends with this line: 'I am told you do not believe in God. I send you God's blessings.'

The great Shaivite mystic of Kashmir, **Lal Ded**—*also known as Lalla Arifa, Lalleshwari and simply Lalla—is revered by Kashmiris of every religious persuasion. In her poems, called vaakhs, she comes across as a powerful and passionate personality. These are two of my favourite vaakhs, in the poet Ranjit Hoskote's excellent translation:*

> Don't torture this body with thirst and hunger,
> Give it a hand when it stumbles and falls.
> To hell with all your vows and prayers:
> Just help others through life, there's no truer worship.

> My Master gave me just one rule:
> Forget the outside, get to the inside of things.
> I, Lalla, took that teaching to heart.
> From that day, I've danced naked.

Do not deceive and do not despise anyone, anywhere.
Do not be angry and do not bear secret resentment;
for, as a mother risks her life
and watches over her child,
so should your love for all things be boundless . . .

Gifts are great, the founding of viharas is meritorious,
meditations and religious practice calm the mind,
understanding of truth, beyond illusions, leads to Nirvana;
but greater than all of these is loving kindness.
As the light of the moon is sixteen times stronger
than the light of all the stars,
so is loving kindness sixteen times more efficacious
in liberating the mind
than all other religious accomplishments taken together.
This state of mind is the best in the world.
Let a man remain steadfast in it while he is awake,
whether he be standing, walking, sitting, or lying down.

~ *The Buddha*
{adapted from a translation by Paul Carus}

Tirthankara **Mahavira**'s *teachings on the sanctity of all life:*

You are that which you intend to hit, injure, insult,
torment, persecute, torture, enslave or kill.

One who neglects or disregards the existence of earth, air,
fire, water and vegetation disregards his own existence
which is entwined with them.

There is nothing so small and subtle as the atom nor any
element so vast as space. Similarly, there is no quality of
soul more subtle than non-violence and no virtue of spirit
greater than reverence for life.

All living beings hate pain, therefore one should not kill or
hurt any living being. Ahimsa is the highest religion.

A wise person does not kill, nor cause others to kill, nor
consent to killings by another.

God is the Master.
God is Truth.
His Name spells love universal.

~ *Guru Nanak*

Do we love our Creator?
Let us love our fellow-beings first.
For God has compassion and loves the compassionate;
And he gives to the mild
What He does not give to the harsh.

~ *Prophet Mohammed*

I say to you that hear, Love your enemies, do good to those
who hate you, bless those who curse you, pray for those
who abuse you. If you love those who love you, what credit
is that to you? For even sinners love those who love them.
And if you do good to those who do good to you, what
credit is that to you? For even sinners do the same.

~ *Jesus*

Kabir, the door of salvation is straight
Narrower than the tenth of the mustard seed.
A man's ego is the size of an elephant
How can he pass through the gate?

~ Kabir

Being wise, know yourself as ignorant
Being strong, know yourself as meek
Being one of modest means, share all the wealth you own:
These are the signs of a true believer.

~ Sheikh Farid

Truly, I say to you, unless you turn and become like
children, you will never enter the kingdom of heaven.
Whoever humbles himself like this child is the greatest in
the kingdom of heaven.

~ Jesus

Ego is a foul disease;
but it carries its own remedy.

~ *Guru Angad*

Lord, make me an instrument of Your peace.
Where there is hatred, let me sow love;
Where there is injury, pardon;
Where there is doubt, faith;
Where there is despair, hope;
Where there is darkness, light;
And where there is sadness, joy.

O Divine master, grant that I may not so much seek
To be consoled, as to console;
To be understood, as to understand;
To be loved, as to love.
For it is in giving that we receive,
It is in pardoning that we are pardoned,
And it is in dying that we are born to eternal life.

Amen.

~ *St Francis of Assisi*

Is there a man who says of all,
Whether upon them sorrow fall
Or whether joy—'These, these are mine'?
That is the saint: mark well the sign,
God dwells in him. The good man's breast
Is of all men's the tenderest.
Is any helpless or undone?
Be he a slave, be he a son—
On all alike he mercy shows,
On all an equal love bestows.

How oft must I this tale repeat!
That man is God's own counterfeit.

~ *Tukaram*
{translation by Nicol Macnicol}

Who is the most favored of Allah?
He from whom the greatest good comes to His creatures.

~ *Prophet Mohammed*

That which is hateful to you, do not do to your fellow.
That is the whole Torah; the rest is the explanation;
go and learn.

~ *Hillel the Elder*

I've lost myself in the city of Love.

I look for myself and this is what I am:
No head, nor limbs, nor feet.
People—who is it that you drag out of my home:
Who will rid you of hate?

I lost my self and found the Self
And all was right with my world.
Bulla's Beloved is Master of heaven and earth;
Everyone is His own; everyone is mine.

~ *Bulle Shah, the Sufi saint-poet of Punjab*
{translation by Sheikh J. Mureed}

In every age and dispensation, all Divine Ordinances are
changed and transformed according to the requirements of
time, except the law of Love.

~ *Bahá'u'lláh*

A great blot on orthodox Hinduism is the caste system and the practice of untouchability. The struggle against this criminal discrimination is centuries old. A number of men and women from the oppressed communities took on the upper castes and came to be regarded as saints. One of the best known is the fifteenth-century saint Ravi Dass, who was from a family of cobblers. He rejected the caste system and preached the equality of all human beings, saying, 'God is everywhere, in you and in me.' His followers today are known as Ravidassias. Some of Sant Ravi Dass's hymns were included in the Sikh holy book, the Guru Granth Sahib, by Guru Arjun Dev.

You are me, and I am You—
what is the difference between us?
We are like gold and the bracelet, or water and the waves.
If I did not commit any sins, O Infinite Lord,
How would You have acquired the name
'Redeemer of sinners'?
You are my Master, the Inner-knower, Searcher of hearts.
The servant is known by his God, and the Lord and Master
is known by His servant.
Grant me the wisdom to worship and adore
You with my body.

O Ravi Dass, one who understands that the Lord is equally
in all, is very rare.

~ *Sant Ravi Dass*
{translation by Nirmal Dass}

Bapu Gandhi *once listed what he considered the Seven Deadly Sins:*

Wealth without work.
Pleasure without conscience.
Science without humanity.
Knowledge without character.
Politics without principle.
Commerce without morality.
Worship without sacrifice.

It is better that you take a rope and gather and bring a bundle of wood upon your back and sell it—in which case God guards your honour—than to beg of people, whether they give you or not.

For if they do not give, you lose your honour and reputation; and if they give, it is much worse than if they do not, for it puts you under obligation.

~ Prophet Mohammed

He who toils and earns,
Then with his hand gives some away,
He, O Nanak, has discovered the True Path.
~ *Guru Nanak*

That man who sows the ground with care and diligence,
He acquires a great stock of religious merit,
Greater than he would gain by ten thousand prayers.
~ *Zarathustra*

Your actions are defined by intention;
Every man shall deserve only that which he intended.
~ *Prophet Mohammed*

The Lord does not look so much at the greatness
of our works—
As at the love with which they are done.
~ *St. Teresa of Ávila*

I discarded the love of self
And the ways of the world,
I gave up distinction between friend and foe
And was blessed with knowledge to recognize the godly.
In the cave of *sahaj* I sat in meditation
Saw the light, heard divine music
And pondered over the word in utter bliss.
I was the blessed bride taken by the Lord.

~ *Guru Arjun Dev*

If a single man conquers in battle one thousand times one
thousand men, and another man conquers himself, the
second man has made the greater conquest.
Conquest of your own self, O Bhikkus, is far better than
victory over other people. Not all the gods in heaven,
nor all the demons in hell, can change into defeat
such a victory.

~ *The Buddha*

The riddle of Creation is solved when you know how
the 'I' was created. So I say, find your Self.

~ *Ramana Maharishi*

Cast off all shame,
and sell yourself
in the marketplace;
then alone
can you hope
to reach the Lord.

Cymbals in hand,
a veena upon my shoulder,
I go about;
who dares to stop me?

The pallav of my sari
falls away (A scandal!);
yet will I enter
the crowded marketplace
without a thought.

Jani says, My Lord,
I have become a slut
to reach Your home.

~ *The Marathi saint-poet Janabai*
{translation by Vilas Sarang}

Guru Gobind Singh, *the last Guru of the Sikhs, suffered hardship and tragedy in life—including the loss of his two young sons, who were executed by his opponents. This verse, one of the few that Guru Gobind wrote in Punjabi, was composed shortly after the killing of his sons and the death of his mother from shock. Even an agnostic like me cannot remain unmoved by this poignant example of faith in extreme adversity:*

> Beloved Friend, beloved God, Thou must hear
> Thy servant's plight. When Thou art not near,
> The comfort's cloak is as a pall of pest,
> The home is like a serpent's nest.
> The wine chokes like the hangman's noose,
> The rim of the goblet is like an assassin's knife;
> But with Thee shall I in adversity dwell.
> Without Thee life of ease is life in hell.

> O God! If I worship You for fear of Hell, burn me in Hell,
> If I worship You in hope of Paradise,
> exclude me from Paradise.
> But if I worship You for Your Own sake,
> grudge me not Your everlasting Beauty.
>
> *~ Rabi'a al-'Adawiyya of Basra, the eighth-century Sufi mystic*

The Yogi dyes his garments, instead of dyeing
His mind in the colours of love:
He sits within the temple of the Lord, leaving Brahma to
worship a stone.
He pierces holes in his ears, he has a great beard
And matted locks, he looks like a goat:
He goes forth into the wilderness, killing all his desires,
And turns himself into a eunuch:
He shaves his head and dyes his garments; he reads the Gita
And becomes a mighty talker.
Kabir says:
'You are going to the doors of death, bound hand and foot!'

~ *Kabir*
{translation by Rabindranath Tagore}

Whether one believes in a religion or not, and whether one
believes in rebirth or not, there isn't anyone who doesn't
appreciate kindness and compassion.

~ *The Dalai Lama*

The simal tree stands tall and straight
But if one comes to it with hope of gain
What will he get and whither turn?
Its fruit is tasteless
Its flowers have no fragrance
Its leaves are of no use.
O Nanak, humility and sweetness
Are the essence of virtue and goodness.
Readily do we all pay homage to ourselves
Before others we refuse to bow.

It is the lowly that have goodness and true worth.
He that bows before all, before him all will bow.

~ *Guru Nanak*

Take care! Rise up from 'me-ness' (and) mix with all!
With the selfness of (your) self, you are (only)
a seed (of grain).
(But together) with all, you are a mine (of jewels).

~ *Maulana Jalaluddin Rumi*
{translation by Ibrahim Gamard}

Good is penance and maceration of the body; but do not
present these to me as a rule for everyone . . .
[Let us] not judge the minds of our fellow creatures,
which are for God alone to judge . . .
When it seems that God shows us
the faults of others, keep on the safer side—
for it may be that thy judgment is false.
On thy lips let silence abide. And any
vice which thou mayest ascribe to others, do thou ascribe at
once to them and to thyself, in true humility. If that vice
really exists in a person, he will correct himself better,
seeing himself so gently understood.

~ *Catherine of Siena*

There is no reason why we should want everyone
to follow our own path . . .
Indiscreet zeal about others must not be indulged in;
it may do us much harm; let each one look to herself . . .
Our souls may lose their peace and even disturb other
people's if we are always criticizing trivial actions which
often are not real defects at all, but we construe them
wrongly through ignorance of their motives.

~ *St Teresa of Ávila*

Everyone asks: 'Lalan, what's your religion in this world?'
Lalan answers: 'How does religion look?'
I've never laid eyes on it.
Some wear malas [Hindu rosaries] around their necks,
some tasbis [Muslim rosaries], and so people say
they've got different religions.
But do you bear the sign of your religion
when you come or when you go?
~ *The Bengali mystic Lalan Fakir*
{translation by Donald Lopez}

For the servant of God there is no caste, no varna,
so say the Vedic sages . . .
He who becomes enraged at the touch of a Mahar is no
Brahmin. There is no penance for him even by giving his
life. There is the taint of untouchability in him who will
not touch a Chandal. Tuka says: A man becomes what he
is continually thinking of.
~ *Tukaram*
{translated by Mahatma Gandhi}

Believe nothing, no matter where you read it, or who said
it—even if I have said it—unless it agrees
with your own reason.
Believe not because some old manuscripts are produced,
believe not because it is your national belief,
believe not because you have been made to
believe from your childhood,
but reason truth out, and after you have analyzed it,
then if you find it will do good to one and all, believe it,
live up to it and help others live up to it.

~ *The Buddha*

The string has snapped, the lute is mute,
The player plays not, his art is gone.
It is all sermons, speeches, talk and idle gossip.
When knowledge comes, he forgets his song.
O Kabir, he who has conquered the five sins,
(Lust, anger, greed, attachment and the ego)
To reach the highest star, he has not far to go.

~ *Kabir*

If a man debates and quarrels about scriptures and
doctrines, he has not tasted the nectar of true faith.

~ *Ramakrishna Paramahansa*

Fool, you won't find your way out by praying from a book.
The perfume on your carcass won't give you a clue.
Focus on the Self.
That's the best advice you can get.

~ *Lal Ded*
{translation by Ranjit Hoskote}

Those killed by the dagger of surrender
Each moment obtain new Life
From the Unseen World.

~ *The eleventh-century Sufi Zinda Pil Sheikh Ahmed Jam*
{translation by Renuka Narayanan}

On the roof, under His moon and exploding stars,
Lucidity's a fool, a fraud, a liar—
The Mystery of Majesty is ringed by darkness
Only the stunned and bewildered ever glimpse the Throne.

~ *Rumi*
{translation by Andrew Harvey}

Two lovely verses where God is a familiar:

Jani sweeps the floor,
The lord collects the dirt,
Carries it upon His head,
And casts it away.
Won over by devotion,
The Lord does lowly chores!
Says Jani to Vithoba,
How shall I pay your debt?

~ *Janabai*
{translation by Vilas Sarang}

Lift your veil now, Beloved, the time to be shy is long past.

That one look from your eyes was a dart
I took it on my heart because you sent it.
You wound me and then you hide your face:
Where do you learn your trickster ways?

Lift your veil now, Beloved, the time to be shy is long past.

~ *Bulle Shah*
{translation by Sheikh J. Mureed}

If there is to be peace in the world,
There must be peace in the nations.

If there is to be peace in the nations,
There must be peace in the cities.

If there is to be peace in the cities,
There must be peace between neighbours.

If there is to be peace between neighbours,
There must be peace in the home.

If there is to be peace in the home,
There must be peace in the heart.

~ Lao Tsu

Our prime purpose in this life is to help others. And if you
can't help them, at least don't hurt them.

~ The Dalai Lama

If we have no peace, it is because we have forgotten that we
belong to each other.

~ Mother Teresa

Mahatma Gandhi, *the man I most admire, on ahimsa, which he defined as non-violence (in word and deed) coupled with honesty:*

Man as animal is violent but as spirit is non-violent.
The moment he awakes to the spirit within he cannot
remain violent. Either he progresses towards
ahimsa or rushes to his doom.

Non-violence is not a garment to be put on and off at will.
Its seat is in the heart, and it must be an inseparable part
of our very being.

So long as one wants to retain one's sword, one has not
attained complete fearlessness.

To take the name of non-violence when there is a sword in
your heart is not only hypocritical and dishonest but cowardly.

The first principle of non-violent action is that of non-cooperation with everything humiliating.

If one has pride and egoism, there is no non-violence. Non-violence is impossible without humility.

If we remain non-violent, hatred will die as everything does, from disuse.

Democracy can only be saved through non-violence, because democracy, so long as it is sustained by violence, cannot provide for or protect the weak. My notion of democracy is that under it the weakest should have the same opportunity as the strongest. This can never happen except through non-violence.

Liberty and democracy become unholy when their hands are dyed red with innocent blood.

The universe is the objective manifestation
of the essence of Shiva.
If you realize this by annihilating your self, you will be
merged into Him.
What will you do after death if you do not realize
Him in this world?
Search for Him in your self and pay heed to what I say.
If you realize God's Unity, Your self shall evaporate.
The light of Unity shines everywhere,
But the intellect cannot grasp it.

~ Hazrat Nuruddin Nurani—also known as Nund Rishi—the
'Muslim Rishi' who best represented Kashmir's syncretic tradition

If God be within the mosque, then to whom
does this world belong?
If Ram be within the image which you find
upon your pilgrimage,
then who is there to know what happens without?
Hari is in the East: Allah is in the West.
Look within your heart,
for there you will find both Karim and Ram;
All the men and women of the world are His living forms.
Kabir is the child of Allah and of Ram:
He is my Guru, He is my Pir.

~ Kabir
{translation by Rabindranath Tagore}

Judge not, that you be not judged. For with the judgment
you pronounce you will be judged, and with the measure
you use it will be measured to you.
Why do you see the speck that is in your brother's eye, but
do not notice the log that is in your own eye? Or how can
you say to your brother, 'Let me take the speck out of your
eye,' when there is the log in your own eye?

~ *Jesus*

There are ignoble amongst the noblest,
And pure amongst the despised.
The former shalt thou avoid.
And be the dust under the foot of the other.

~ *Guru Nanak*

Once, I set out to find the crooked of heart and
returned disappointed.
Then I looked into my heart: I found the king of crooks
hiding there.

~ *Kabir*

When I see a person who has been given more than me
in money and beauty,
Let me look to those who have been given less;
Let me think of those worse off than me,
That I may not hold God's benefits in contempt.

~ Prophet Mohammed

Farid believed he alone was stricken with sorrow
But sorrow is spread over the entire world;
I climbed my roof and whichever way I turned
I saw that every home in sorrow burned.
Therefore be kind;
Therefore don't wallow in self pity.

~ Sheikh Farid

In order to be All, do not desire to be anything.
In order to know All, do not desire to know anything.
In order to find the joy of All,
do not desire to enjoy anything.

~ John of the Cross

There is no greater virtue before God than prayer, and
prayer is in hearing the complaints of the aggrieved and
assisting them, in helping the needy and the oppressed, in
feeding the hungry and in bringing liberty to the captive.

*~ The great sufi saint of the subcontinent, Khwaja Muinuddin
Chishti, also known as Gharib Nawaz or Benefactor of the Poor*

Learn to see the Divine in every human being.
Give food to the hungry and water to the thirsty and
clothes to the naked. This is how you please God.
Know that those who give food to any creature suffering
the pangs of hunger are, in fact, feeding God.

~ Shirdi Sai Baba

Make us worthy, Lord, to serve our fellow men
throughout the world who live and die
in poverty and hunger.
Give them through our hands this day their daily bread,
and by our understanding love, give peace and joy.

~ Mother Teresa

The throbbing of every heart He hears
Pain of the good and wicked He knows;
From the tiny ant to the mighty elephant
He casts a benign look on all and is content.
~ *Guru Gobind Singh*

[God] sees and hears all.
He dwells in the recesses of our hearts.
Even the ones who show Him no gratitude
Are helped by Him.
Nanak's God is ever forgiving.
~ *Guru Arjun Dev*

To see the universal and all-pervading Spirit of Truth
face to face, one must be able to love the meanest of
creation as oneself.
~ *Mahatma Gandhi*

Not abstinence from fish or flesh,
not going naked, not shaving the head,
not matted hair, not rough or torn garments,
not covering oneself with dirt, not sacrificing to Agni—
nothing will cleanse a man who is not free from delusions.

~ *The Buddha*

Some worship stones and on their heads they bear them;
Some the phallus, strung in necklaces, wear as an emblem.
Some behold their god in the south,
some to the west bow their head.
The world is thus bound in false ritual
And God's secret is still unread.

~ *Guru Gobind Singh*

They say: Pilgrim, come to Mathura;
to Dwarka, Kashi, Haridwar—
Ravi Dass, I journeyed deep into myself,
and found the Beloved there.

~ *Ravi Dass*

O pundit, your hair-splitting's
So much bullshit. I'm surprised
You still get away with it.

If parroting the name
Of Rama brought salvation,
Then saying *sugarcane*
Should sweeten the mouth,
Saying *fire* burn the feet,
Saying *water* slake thirst,
And saying *food*
Would be as good as a belch.

If saying *money* made everyone rich,
There'd be no beggars in the streets.

My back is turned on the world,
You hear me singing of Rama and you smile.
One day, Kabir says,
All bundled up,
You'll be delivered to Deathville.

~ *Kabir*
{translation by Arvind Krishna Mehrotra}

Running up minarets,
Calling out to the faithful
Five times a day,
What's your problem, muezzin?

Can't you see you're a walking
Mosque yourself?
Your mind's your Mecca;
Your body the Ka'aba
That you face when you pray;
Anything you say
Is an utterance from heaven.
Cut the throat of desire,
Not a poor goat's, if you must.

Kabir says, I'm possessed,
Just don't ask me how
It happened or when.

~ *Kabir*
{translation by Arvind Krishna Mehrotra}

Chant only the name of Hari,
Be humble, lighter than a straw in the dust
Be tolerant and generous as a shade-giving tree
Empty yourself of all pride and honour others.
And then [again] chant the name of Hari.

~ Chaitanya Mahaprabhu

Break down the mosque, break down the temple
Break down whatever there is besides;
But never break a human heart
That is where God Himself resides.

~ Bulle Shah

Seeking the truth, I went to the scholars of the Vedas
And found them full of 'You shall' and 'You shall not'.
They had neither knowledge nor peace,
Their minds bloated to distress with the mighty 'I'.

~ Namdev

Sufis, Bhakti saints, the Sikh Gurus and many Christian mystics believed in complete surrender to God—the Beloved, or husband, or simply Love. They used the language of earthly love, sometimes of erotic longing and union, to express their devotion. In the process they composed beautiful and passionate sacred verse. Over the next few pages are examples of such mystic-love poetry.

Only he whose garment is rent by the violence of love
Is wholly pure from covetousness and sin.
Hail to thee, then, O Love, sweet madness!
Thou who healest all our infirmities!
Who art the physician of our pride and self-conceit!

. . .

[Should] my Beloved only touch me with his lips,
I, too, like the flute, would burst out in melody . . .
The Beloved is all in all, the lover only veils Him;
The Beloved is all that lives, the lover a dead thing.
How can I retain my senses about me,
When the Beloved shows not the light of His countenance?
Love desires that His [Mystery] should be revealed [in me],
For if a mirror reflects not, of what use is it?

~ *Rumi*
{adapted from a translation by E.H. Whinfield}

My merits and demerits You did not reckon
Nor looked upon my face, complexion or adornment.
I knew no winsome ways nor manner of deportment
But You took me by the hand and drew me to your bed.
Listen, my friends—My Groom has become my Master,
He puts his hand upon my forehead and calls me His own.
What know the foolish men of the world?
Now has my union been consummated
My Groom knows my sorrows and has dispelled them.
The moonlight shines in my courtyard
Night and day I live in ecstasy with my Love.
My raiments are redder than the rose
I glitter with jewels and garlands of flowers.
My Love looks at me and I have the wealth of the world.
I have no fear of the wicked demons.
I am eternally Happy and full of joy—
I have found Truth in my home.

~ Guru Arjun Dev

Late have I loved you, O Beauty ever ancient, ever new,
late have I loved you! You were within me, but I was
outside, and it was there that I searched for you. In my
unloveliness, I plunged into the lovely things which you
created. You were with me, but I was not with you. Created
things kept me from you; yet if they had not been in you
they would not have been at all. You called, you shouted,
and you broke through my deafness. You flashed, you
shone, and you dispelled my blindness. You breathed your
fragrance on me; I drew in breath and now I pant for you.
I have tasted you, now I hunger and thirst for more. You
touched me, and I burned for your peace.

~ Augustine

How She first made me beautiful promises
And then grew cruel, I now know.
That Love did not deceive or mock me
In that woe, would I might understand it!
But She meant to make clear
And reveal to me
How reason illuminates the entire abyss of Love.

~ Hadewijch of Antwerp, the thirteenth-century Flemish mystic
{translation by Mother Columba Hart}

O Farid, the lane is slushy with mud,
The House of The One you love is far away.
If you go, it will soak your cloak,
If you stay, it will sunder your love.

I'll let my cloak be soaked.
'Tis Allah who makes the rain come down in torrents.
I will go forth to seek my Beloved,
The bonds of our love will not sever.

~ *Sheikh Farid*

He walked past my door
Dressed as a beggar, He
With shining hair and gleaming teeth,
Unconcerned. He drew me out
I went after Him, I took Him by the hand—
He woke me up, my Lord Chenna Mallikeshwara.

~ *Akka Mahadevi*
{translation by Samyukta Dutt}

O Love's living flame,
Tenderly you wound
My soul's deepest centre!
Since you no longer evade me,
Will you, please, at last conclude:
Rend the veil of this sweet encounter!

O cautery so tender!
O pampered wound!
O soft hand! O touch so delicately strange,
Tasting of eternal life
And cancelling all debts!
Killing, death into life you change!

~ *John of the Cross*
{translation by Antonio T. de Nicolas}

After abducting me if now Thou dost not embrace me,
where is Thy chivalry, Oh Arunachala?
Enfold me body to body, limb to limb, or I am lost,
Oh Arunachala!

~ *Ramana Maharishi*
{translation by Ramanasramam}

My friend, I've bought up
Govind. Did you say
it was done
in hiding?
I took him beating my drum.

Did you say
he came
expensive? I tell you,
I weighed all
upon the scales

and then I gave
my body, my life, and things
like that.

Let me,
says Meera,
see you.

You said so,
a life ago.

~ *Meera Bai*
{translation by Shama Futehally}

O mullah, don't call me to prayer
Let me serve and please my Beloved.
I'm a harlot, I lose no honour
Let me dance and please my Beloved.
People can figure out the price of love
I'll wear His garland and be His bride.
Says Bulle Shah, to Him, His ways
Let me keep my vows of love.

~ *Bulle Shah*

Fair mothers, my sweet ambrosia
Of Srirangam
With his lovely hair, his lovely mouth
His lovely eyes
And the lovely lotus from his belly button—
My husband—
Has my loose bangle
Made me lose indeed!

~ *A love-hymn to Vishnu by Andal, the only female Alvar saint*
{translation by Paula Marvelly}

She whose heart is full of love
Is ever in full bloom.
Joy is hers for she has no love of self.
Only those who love You
Conquer love of self.
Come, Lord, and abide in me.

Many a garment did I wear,
The Master willed not and
His place was barred to me.
When he wanted me, I went
With garlands and strings of jewels
and with raiment of finery.

Nanak says: A bride welcomed in the Master's mansion
Has found true Love.

~ Guru Nanak

A hymn to Vishnu by the Tamil Vaishnava saint **Nammalvar**.
The translation is by A.K. Ramanujan:

My dark one
stands there as if nothing's changed
after taking entire
into his maw
all three worlds
the gods
and the good kings
who hold their lands
as a mother would
a child in her womb—

and I
by his leave
have taken him entire

and I have him in my belly
for keeps.

I speak the Truth for everyone to hear:
Only those who learn to love will find the Lord.
—*Guru Gobind Singh*

Go and wash off all hatred from your chest
Seven times with water.
Then you can become our companion
Drinking from the wine of love.

~ *Rumi*
{translation by Rasoul Sorkhabi}

Holiness is not a luxury for the few; it is not just for some
people. It is meant for you and for me, for all of us.
It is a simple duty, because if we learn to love,
we learn to be holy.

~ *Mother Teresa*

I do not keep the Hindu fast, nor the Muslim Ramadan.
I serve Him alone who is my refuge.
I serve the One Master, who is also Allah.
I have broken with the Hindu and the Muslim,
I will not worship with the Muslim,
nor like the Muslim go to Mecca,
I shall serve Him and no other.
I will not pray to idols nor say the Muslim prayer.
I shall put my heart at the feet of the One Supreme Being;
For we are [all one,] neither Hindus nor Mussalmans.

~ *Guru Arjun Dev*

Ice, frozen water and snow, all these
have been created by God.
They all appear different, but are of the same essence.
When the rays of the sun fall upon them,
They all turn into water.

~ *Hazrat Nuruddin Nurani, or Nund Rishi,*
on the unity of all mankind

To love only members of the Brahmo Samaj
is maya [delusion].
To love only members of one's own family is maya.
To love only one's own countrymen is maya.
But to love the people of all countries is daya [compassion].
To love the followers of all religions is daya.
Such love comes from love of God, who is daya.

~ *Ramakrishna Paramahamsa*

Devotion to Allah is of two kinds: jazmi and mutta-adi.
In jazmi devotion, benefit accrues to the devotee alone.
This type of devotion includes regular prescribed prayers,
fasting, pilgrimage to Mecca and telling the beads of the
rosary. Mutta-adi devotion, on the other hand, brings
advantage and comfort to oneself and others. It is
performed by spending money on others, showing
affection to people and by always striving to help one's
fellow human beings. The reward of mutta-adi devotion
is endless and limitless . . .

Divine bounty does not discriminate between one
individual and another. When the sun rises, it gives light
and warmth to all people, whether they live in palaces or in
huts. When it rains, it falls alike on the poor and rich, and
both benefit from it.

~ *Nizamuddin Auliya*

When one's acts are righteous
Learning and knowledge follow.
When the five senses are mastered
Life becomes a pilgrimage.
When the heart is in tune [with the Almighty]
Then tinkle the dancer's ankle-bells.
What can Yama do
When I am in unison with You?

He who abandons desires,
He is the real Sanyasi.
He who has mastered passions
Has become a true yogi.
He who has compassion
Is the true monk,
For he has killed his self without killing himself.

~ *Guru Nanak*

Religious experience is usually associated with extreme austerity and penance. But prophets and saints have also spoken about the need to be happy and the importance of physical and mental well-being:

You, yourself, as much as anybody in the entire universe,
deserve your love and affection . . .
To satisfy the necessities of life is not evil.
To keep the body in good health is a duty, for otherwise
we shall not be able to trim the lamp of wisdom,
and keep our mind strong and clear.
~ *The Buddha*

I do not know whether the universe with its countless galaxies, stars and planets has a deeper meaning or not, but at the very least, it is clear that we humans who live on this earth face the task of making a happy life for ourselves . . . From my limited experience, I have found that the greatest degree of inner tranquility comes from the development of love and compassion. The more we care for the happiness of others, the greater our sense of well-being becomes.
~ *The Dalai Lama*

Those who consider themselves happy and whose sense of
power depends on the idea that they are beyond suffering
any evil are not able to have mercy on others.

~ *St Thomas Aquinas*

In destruction there is no victory but for darkness.
The power of victory is not force but Love . . .
As light disperses darkness, so does Love swallow up
hatred, and it is no more.

~ *Jesus*

It is easy enough to be friendly to one's friends. But to
befriend the one who regards himself as your enemy is the
quintessence of true religion. The other is mere business.

~ *Mahatma Gandhi*

The earth is but one country and mankind its citizens.

~ *Bahá'u'lláh*

When I despair,
I remember that all through history,
the ways of truth and love have always won.
There have been tyrants, and murderers,
and for a time they can seem invincible,
but in the end they always fall.
Think of this, always.

~ *Mahatma Gandhi*

Men must speak the truth,
The truth living in their thoughts,
Not have a promise on their lips
And a lie in their hearts.

~ *Guru Gobind Singh in the* Zafarnama
{translation by Navtej Sarna}

There was Truth in the beginning,
There was Truth before the Aeons.
There is Truth now, Nanak,
And there will be Truth hereafter.

~ *Guru Nanak*

The most excellent Holy War is that for the conquest of self;
Therefore, let God fill my angry heart with safety and faith;
For no person has drunk a better draught than one
Who has swallowed anger for God's dear sake.

~ *Prophet Mohammed*

Fight with yourself, why fight with external foes?
He who conquers himself through himself,
will obtain happiness.
Know thyself, recognize thyself, be immersed in thyself:
Thus will you attain Godhood . . .
Every soul is in itself omniscient and blissful.
Bliss does not come from anywhere outside.

~ *Mahavira*

He who knows others is learned;
He who knows himself is wise.

~ *Lao Tsu*

Of the many 'Precepts of Mind Training' that the Fourteenth
Dalai Lama has given us, here are some that make the most sense
to me. The Dalai Lama has derived these from the teachings of the
twelfth-century Buddhist teacher Geshe Chekawa:

Don't speak of others' faults.
Don't concern yourself with others' business.
Don't make malicious banter.
Don't lie in ambush.
Don't strike at the heart.
Don't sprint to win the race.
Don't place the load of a horse on a pony.
Don't seek others' misery as a means to happiness.
Don't apply a wrong understanding.
Don't be boastful.
Don't be short-tempered.
Don't make a short-lived attempt.
Don't expect gratitude.

If you say that the abode of the Gods is in the sky,
the birds will arrive there before you. If you say it is in the sea,
the fish will arrive there before you.
Know that the heavenly realm is both inside you and
outside you, and you will know that which is outside by
that which is inside.
When you have found the Light within yourselves, you will
know as you are known. Then you will know that you are
the children of the Living Parents and that your destiny
is to be as they are.
The person who knows not himself, is poor in Spirit,
for he is his own poverty.

~ *Jesus*

He knows the crown is the temple of Self.
His breath is deepened by the Unstruck Sound.
He has freed himself from the prison of delusion.
He knows he is God, who shall He worship?

~ *Lal Ded*
{translation by Ranjit Hoskote}

If you seek yourself elsewhere (outside of yourself), how can
you ever find yourself?
This is just like an idiot going into a crowd of many people,
and having let himself become confused because of the
spectacle, [he] does not recognize himself; and, even
though he searches for himself everywhere, he continually
makes the error of mistaking others for himself...
Since you do not see the natural condition of the real
disposition of things, you do not know that appearances
come from the mind, and so you are thrust
once again into Samsara.
By not seeing that your own mind is actually the Buddha,
Nirvana becomes obscured.

~ *Padmasambhava*
{translation by John Myrdhin Reynolds}

Go into your hearts, it is the greatest pilgrimage
One heart is better than a thousand Kaabas.

~ *Rumi*

How long will you keep pounding on an open door
begging for someone to open it?
~ *Rabi'a al-'Adawiyya*

If you are seeking Allah,
Then keep clear of religious formalities.
Those who have seen Allah
Are away from all religions!
Those who do not see Allah here,
How will they see Him beyond?

Let us go to the land of Kak
Where love flows in abundance,
There are no entrances, no exits,
Every one can see the Lord!
~ *Shah Abdul Latif Bhitai of Sindh*
{translation by D.H. Butani}

Without goodness, prayer has no meaning.

~ *Guru Amar Das*

[Do not] love your neighbour for your own profit,
for that would not be faithful love;
And you would then not respond to the love which
the Lord bears you.
As the Lord has loved you of grace, so He wills that since
you cannot return this love to Him,
You should return it to your neighbour,
loving him of grace and not by barter.

~ *Catherine of Siena*

If we can enter the church day and night and implore God
to hear our prayers, how careful we should be to hear and
grant the petitions of our neighbours in need.

~ *St Francis of Assisi*

God is not merciful to him who is not so to mankind.

~ *Prophet Mohammed*

He who in adversity grieves not;
He who is without fear;
He who falls not in the snare of sensuality;
Who has no greed for gold, knowing it is like dust.
He who does not slander people when their backs are turned
Nor flatters them to their faces.
He who has neither gluttony in his heart
Nor vanity, nor attachment with worldly things.
He whom nothing moves,
Neither good fortune nor ill,
Who cares not for world's applause,
Nor its censure,
Who ignores every wishful fantasy
And accepts what comes his way as it comes.
He whom lust cannot lure
Nor anger command,
In such a one lives God Himself.

~ *Guru Tegh Bahadur*

We need to find God, and he cannot be found in noise
and restlessness. God is the friend of silence. See how
nature—trees, flowers, grass—grows in silence; see the stars,
the moon and the sun, how they move in silence . . .
We need silence to be able to touch souls.

~ *Mother Teresa*

My Beloved is the mountains,
And lovely wooded valley,
Strange islands,
And resounding rivers,
The whistling of love-stirring breezes.
The tranquil night
At the time of the rising dawn,
Silent music [.]

~ *John of the Cross*

If you have men who will exclude any of God's creatures
from the shelter of compassion and pity, you will have men
who will deal likewise with their fellow men.

~ *St Francis of Assisi*

God, help me acquire knowledge, to teach me right from
wrong, to light the path to heaven, to be my friend in the
desert, my society in solitude, my friend when friendless,
my guide to happiness, to sustain me in misery:
for knowledge is an ornament amongst friends and
an armour against enemies.

~ *Prophet Mohammed*

Ye ask, who are those that draw us to the kingdom
if the kingdom is in Heaven?

. . . the fowls of the air and all beasts that are under
the earth or upon the earth and the fishes of the sea,
these are they which draw you
and the kingdom of Heaven is within you
and whosoever shall know himself shall find it.

Strive therefore to know yourselves and ye shall be aware
that ye are the sons of the Almighty Father; and ye shall
know that ye are in the city of God and ye are the city.

~ *Jesus*

Let's go!
Everyone keeps saying,
As if they knew where paradise is,
But ask them what lies beyond
The street they live on,
They'll give you a blank look.

If paradise is where they're heading,
Paradise is not where they'll end up.
And what if the talk of paradise is just hearsay?
You better check out the place yourself.
As for me, says Kabir, if you're listening,
Good company's all I seek.

~ Kabir
{translation by Arvind Krishna Mehrotra}

When your heart's clean and right
The Ganga's in your bath tub.

~ Ravi Dass

Behold but One in all things;
it is the second that leads you astray.

~ *Kabir*

In samadhi one attains the knowledge of Brahman—one
realizes Brahman. In that state reasoning stops altogether,
and man becomes mute. He has no power to describe
the nature of Brahman.
Once a salt doll went to measure the depth of the ocean.
It wanted to tell others how deep the water was. But this it
could never do, for no sooner did it get into the water than
it melted. Now who was there to report the ocean's depth?

~ *Ramakrishna Paramahamsa*

You go running into temples and mosques
But you never step inside your own mind.
You do battle with the devil every day, to no avail
But you won't gird up and wrestle with your ego.
Bulle Shah, how you trap the swift creatures of the sky!
But you can't grasp the One who sits still in your home.

~ *Bulle Shah*

Drukpa Kunley, *Bhutan's 'Divine Madman', is the most unconventional holy man the world has known. His anecdotes are ribald beyond belief, and he often said, 'The best chung wine lies at the bottom of the pail / And Happiness lies below the navel.' Wherever he went, he carried his 'divine thunderbolt of wisdom' (his penis) before him. It penetrated the mysteries of life as it did willing virgins. The bawdy tales of fornication and copious intake of chung are interspersed with advice on how to square one's karma and attain nirvana. Here is one of his teachings (translated by Keith Dowman and Sonam Paljor):*

Although the clitoris is suitably triangular,
It is ineligible as devil-food for the local god's worship.
Although love-juice can never dry up in the sun,
It is unsuited for tea to quench thirst.
Although a scrotum can hang very low,
It is an unsuitable bag for the hermitage's victuals.
Although a penis has a sound shaft and a large head,
It is not a hammer to strike a nail.
Though endowed with a human body and shapely,
It is not proper to be mistress to the Lord of Death.
Although your mind may be virtuous and pure,
The Buddhas' Teaching is not accomplished by
staying at home.
The teaching of the Tantric Mysteries is most profound,
But liberation cannot be gained
without profound experience.
Drukpa Kunley may show you the way,
But you must traverse the path by yourself.

When you are destitute,
Trade with Allah through charity.
~ *Hazrat Ali*

Whosoever destroys a soul, it is considered as if he
destroyed an entire world. And whosoever saves a life, it is
considered as if he saved an entire world.
~ *Hillel the Elder*

If you have a particular faith or religion, that is good.
But you can survive without it . . .
There is no need for temples, no need for complicated
philosophies. My brain and my heart are my temples; my
philosophy is kindness.
~ *The Dalai Lama*

PHILOSOPHERS,
POETS
and
OTHER
WORDSMITHS

.....

While I have enjoyed reading the different scriptures and found some good prose and poetry in them, given a choice I would rather read the work of great writers, poets and dramatists like Kalidas, Shakespeare, Keats, Goethe, Ghalib, Tagore, Iqbal, Eliot and Faiz. The best literature has the power to alter us, usually for the better. Great writers have a rare gift, which even they don't fully understand or control—the gift of insight. They can look into the heart of the human condition. And if we follow their gaze, we become stronger, humbler, wiser, more attuned to life, or at least more able to appreciate and cope with it.

Poetry and poetic prose, especially, can also fill us with wonder at life, at nature and at the human experience. It can have a hypnotic effect. It is no surprise that many great mystics were also accomplished poets.

Besides poetry and prose, this section includes observations on life and faith by philosophers—from ancients like Confucius to modern thinkers like Bertrand Russell. Philosophy has got a bad name because of its worst practitioners who take pride in bamboozling people with big words and complex sentences. The best philosophers, however, excelled at pithy observations. I strongly believe the study of the world's major philosophers should be made mandatory in schools.

These are the opening lines of Bapu Gandhi's favourite bhajan, 'Vaishnava jana', composed by the Gujarati poet-saint **Narsinh Mehta**:

> Know them alone as the people of God
> Who know the pain of another.
> They help those in need, and share their sorrows,
> But their hearts are free of pride.
> They honour all that lives in this world
> And hurt no one with harsh judgement.
> They are calm of mind, in word and deed;
> Blessed the mothers who birth them.

For everything that lives is holy, life delights in life.

~ *William Blake*

For what
shall I handle a dagger,
O Lord?

What shall I pull it out of,
or stab it in,

when You are all the world,
O Ramanatha?

~ *The Virashaiva Kannada poet Devara Daasimayya*
{translation by A.K. Ramanujan}

Lord, take my lips and speak through them;
take my mind and think through it;
take my heart and set it on fire.

~ *W.H.H. Aitken*

Not in temples nor in mosques,
He makes His home in all creation.
The universe is submerged in His essence.
The wise are drowned in His love.

~ *Sarmad, the fakir who described himself as 'a sufi, a pundit, a
Buddhist monk, a rabbi, an infidel and a Muslim', and roamed the
streets of Delhi naked. He was beheaded by Aurangzeb for heresy.*

Pax

All that matters is to be at one with the living God
to be a creature in the house of the God of Life.

Like a cat asleep on a chair
at peace, in peace
and at one with the master of the house, with the mistress,
at home, at home in the house of the living,
sleeping on the hearth, and yawning before the fire.

Sleeping on the hearth of the living world,
yawning at home before the fire of life
feeling the presence of the living God
like a great reassurance
a deep calm in the heart
a presence
as of the master sitting at the board
in his own and greater being,
in the house of life.

~ D.H. *Lawrence*

I am the Truth (*An-al-Haq*).

~ The tenth-century Sufi poet and philosopher Mansur Al-Hallaj. He paid for this statement with his life: he was executed for blasphemy.

O Me! O life! . . . of the questions of these recurring;
Of the endless trains of the faithless—of cities fill'd
with the foolish;
Of myself forever reproaching myself (for who more foolish
than I, and who more faithless?);
Of eyes that vainly crave the light—of the objects mean—
of the struggle ever renew'd;
Of the poor results of all—of the plodding and sordid
crowds I see around me;
Of the empty and useless years of the rest—
with the rest me intertwined;
The question, O me! so sad, recurring—
What good amid these, O me, O life?

Answer:
That you are here—that life exists, and identity;
That the powerful play goes on,
and you will contribute a verse.

~ Walt Whitman

I bow to that radiance,
peaceful and still,
endless, unbound
by space and time,
which is the spirit,
and only known
through self-awareness.

~ *Bhartrihari*
{translation by A.N.D. Haksar}

Nowhere did I see the Splendour
That I saw in the cave of my heart,
Many times I dashed my head in the mosque
Many times in the temple of idols Him I sought.

~ *Bahadur Shah Zafar*

Know thyself.

~ *Socrates*

Divine Image

For Mercy, Pity, Peace, and Love
Is God, our father dear,
And Mercy, Pity, Peace, and Love
Is Man, his child and care.

For Mercy has a human heart,
Pity a human face,
And Love, the human form divine,
And Peace, the human dress.

Then every man, of every clime,
That prays in his distress,
Prays to the human form divine,
Love, Mercy, Pity, Peace.

And all must love the human form,
In Heathen, Turk, or Jew;
Where Mercy, Love, and Pity dwell
There God is dwelling too.

~ *William Blake*

He prayeth well, who loveth well
Both man and bird and beast.

He prayeth best, who loveth best
All things both great and small [.]

~ *Samuel Taylor Coleridge,*
'The Rime of the Ancient Mariner'

Non-attachment is not indifference
Or shrinking from the world of men;
Nor does renunciation justify
Estrangement from our fellow-men . . .
If to thee life seems to be
A waste and wilderness,
Then shun thine ego; it is the source
Of thine unhappiness.
Shun not thy fellow-men.

~ *Mirza Ghalib*
{translation by J.L. Kaul}

Drink wine, tear up the holy book,
set fire to the house of God,
Go make your house in a temple full of idols;
You may do all these, but do not hurt a man.

~ *Hafiz*

Love is God, as God is Love itself;
The two are one, like sun and sunshine.

~ *Ras Khan (Syed Ibrahim Khan),*
the medieval Krishna bhakt of Mathura

If I can stop one heart from breaking,
I shall not live in vain;
If I can ease one life the aching,
Or cool one pain,
Or help one fainting robin
Unto his nest again,
I shall not live in vain.

~ *Emily Dickinson*

The quality of mercy is not strained
It droppeth as the gentle rain from heaven
Upon the place beneath: it is twice blessed;
It blesseth him that gives and him that takes:
'Tis mightiest in the mightiest; it becomes
The throned monarch better than his crown;
His scepter shows the force of temporal power,
The attribute to awe and majesty,
Wherein doth sit the dread and fear of kings;
But mercy is above the sceptred sway
It is enthroned in the hearts of kings
It is an attribute of God himself,
And earthly power doth then show likest God's
When mercy seasons justice.

~ *Shakespeare*, The Merchant of Venice

All, everything that I understand, I understand only
because I love.

~ *Leo Tolstoy*

Where the mind is without fear and the head is held high;
Where knowledge is free;
Where the world has not been broken up into fragments
by narrow domestic walls;
Where words come out from the depth of truth;
Where tireless striving stretches its arm towards perfection;
Where the clear stream of reason has not lost its way into
the dreary desert sand of dead habit;
Where the mind is led forward by
Thee into ever-widening thought and action—
Into that freedom of heaven, my Father,
let my country awake.

~ *from Rabindranath Tagore's* Gitanjali

Steel your will with such power
That at every turn of fate it be so
That God should ask of his slave,
'Tell me, what is it that pleases you?'

~ *Muhammad Iqbal*

Out of the night that covers me,
Black as the pit from pole to pole,
I thank whatever gods may be
For my unconquerable soul.

In the fell clutch of circumstance
I have not winced nor cried aloud.
Under the bludgeonings of chance
My head is bloody, but unbowed.

~ W.E. Henley, '*Echoes*'

Salute the gods? But even they
cannot escape relentless fate.
Salute that fate? But even it
bears fruit to deeds proportionate.
Then, if fruit depends on deeds,
are gods and fate of any avail?
Salutations to deeds on which
even fate cannot prevail.

~ Anonymous Sanskrit poet in Subhashitavali, *a verse anthology
compiled by Vallabhadeva in fifteenth-century Kashmir*
{translation by A.N.D. Haksar}

No coward soul is mine,
No trembler in the world's storm-troubled sphere:
I see Heaven's glories shine,
And faith shines equal, arming me from fear.

O God within my breast,
Almighty, ever-present Deity!
Life—that in me has rest,
As I—undying Life—have power in Thee!

Vain are the thousand creeds
That move men's hearts: unutterably vain;
Worthless as withered weeds,
Or idlest froth amid the boundless main . . .
With wide-embracing love
Thy spirit animates eternal years,
Pervades and broods above,
Changes, sustains, dissolves, creates, and rears.
Though earth and man were gone,
And suns and universes ceased to be,
And Thou were left alone,
Every existence would exist in Thee.

~*from 'Last Lines' by Emily Brontë*

Come to us, Spirit of Knowledge,
Come, fire us with courage.
And those who fret in misery,
Deliver them across the Sea of Suffering,
Spear-holder,
Beautiful One!

~ A popular prayer, addressed to Shiva's son Kartikeya,
or Murugan, by the Tamil poet Subramanya Bharati
{translation by Renuka Narayanan}

This above all—to thine own self be true;
And it must follow, as night the day,
Thou canst not then be false to any man.

~ Shakespeare, Hamlet

May God bring a storm in your life,
There is no agitation in the waves of your life's ocean.

~ Muhammad Iqbal

Disturb us, Lord, when
We are too well pleased with ourselves,
When our dreams have come true
Because we have dreamed too little,
When we arrived safely
Because we sailed too close to the shore.

Disturb us, Lord, when
With the abundance of things we possess
We have lost our thirst
For the waters of life;
Having fallen in love with life,
We have ceased to dream of eternity
And in our efforts to build a new earth,
We have allowed our vision
of the new Heaven to dim.

Disturb us, Lord, to dare more boldly,
To venture on wider seas
Where storms will show your mastery;
Where losing sight of land,
We shall find the stars.

~ *Sir Francis Drake*

Let us not confine ourselves to prostrating ourselves before
the tree of creation, and to the contemplation of its
branches full of stars. We have a duty to labour over the
human soul, to defend the mystery against the miracle, to
adore the incomprehensible and reject the absurd, to
admit, as an inexplicable fact, only what is necessary, to
purify belief, to remove superstitions from above religion;
to clear God of caterpillars.

~ *Victor Hugo*

This is the excellent foppery of the world, that when we are
sick in fortune (often the surfeits of our own behaviour) we
make guilty of our disasters the sun, the moon, and stars:
as if we were villains on necessity; fools by heavenly
compulsion; knaves, thieves, and treacherous by spherical
predominance; drunkards, liars, and adulterers by an
enforced obedience of planetary influence; and all that we
are evil in, by a divine thrusting on.
An admirable evasion of whoremaster man,
to lay his goatish disposition on the charge of a star!

—*Shakespeare,* King Lear

Alike for those who for To-day prepare,
And those that after To-morrow stare,
A muezzin from the Tower of Darkness cries,
'Fools! your Reward is neither Here nor There!'

~ *Omar Khayyam,* The Rubaiyat
{translation by Edward Fitzgerald}

Lay not reproach at the drunkard's door
O Fanatic, you who are 'pure of soul';
Not for you on the page of life to enrol
The faults of others! Or [whether] less or more
I have swerved from my path—keep to your own;
For every man when he reaches the goal
Shall reap the harvest his hands have sown.

~ *Hafiz*
{adapted from a translation by Gertrude Bell}

With the preacher of morality I had no truck;
I did not waste my life, I had good luck.

~ *Faiz Ahmed Faiz*

Your spirit is a river. Its sacred ghat is contemplation; its
waters are truth; its banks are godliness; its waves are love.
Go to that river to cleanse your soul,
mere water will do nothing for you.

~ *from Narayana's* Hitopadesa

Will the application of white ashes do away
with the smell of a wine pot?
Will a cord over your neck make you twice-born?
What are you the better for smearing your body with ashes?
Your thoughts should set on God alone; for the rest,
an ass can wallow in dirt as well as you.

The books that are called the Vedas are like courtesans,
deluding men, and wholly unfathomable; but the hidden
knowledge of God is like an honourable wife.
O ye asses! why do you make balls of food and give them to
the crow to be an ancestor of yours?

He that fasts shall become (in his next birth) a village pig;
he that embraces poverty shall become a beggar; and he
that bows to a stone shall become a lifeless image.

~ *Vemana, a famous Telugu poet of the seventeenth century*
{translation by C.P. Brown}

Leave this chanting and singing and
telling of beads! Whom dost thou
worship in this lonely dark corner of a
temple with doors all shut? Open
thine eyes and see thy God is not before thee!
He is there where the tiller is tilling
the hard ground and where the path maker
is breaking stones. He is with
them in sun and in shower, and his
garment is covered with dust. Put off
thy holy mantle and even like him come
down on the dusty soil!

~ from Rabindranath Tagore's Gitanjali

Give the rich respect and glory as they prize—
And fob off the poor with promises of paradise!

~ Urdu poet Abdul Hameed Adam

Work is love made visible.
And if you cannot work with love but only with distaste,
it is better that you should leave your work and sit at the
gate of the temple and take alms of those
who work with joy.
For if you bake bread with indifference, you bake a bitter
bread that feeds but half man's hunger.

And if you grudge the crushing of the grapes, your grudge
distills a poison in the wine.
And if you sing though as angels, and love not the singing,
you muffle man's ears to the voices of the day
and the voices of the night.

~ *Kahlil Gibran*

The end of life is life. Life is action, the use of one's powers.
And to use them to their height is our joy and duty.

~ *American jurist Oliver Wendell Homes Jr, often referred to as
'The Great Dissenter'*

We have to do the best we can. This is our sacred
human responsibility.

~ *Albert Einstein*

Gerard Manley Hopkins, *the Victorian poet and Jesuit priest, composed some of the best poetry in the English language. But he never published any because he believed it would violate the vow of humility demanded by his faith.*

God's Grandeur

The world is charged with the grandeur of God.
It will flame out, like shining from shook foil;
It gathers to a greatness, like the ooze of oil
Crushed. Why do men then now not reck his rod?
Generations have trod, have trod, have trod;
And all is seared with trade; bleared, smeared with toil;
And wears man's smudge and shares man's smell: the soil
Is bare now, nor can foot feel, being shod.

And for all this, nature is never spent;
There lives the dearest freshness deep down things;
And though the last lights off the black West went
Oh, morning, at the brown brink eastward, springs—
Because the Holy Ghost over the bent
World broods with warm breast and with ah! bright wings.

O Beauty! dost thou generate
from Heaven or from Hell?
Within thy glance, so diabolic and divine,
Confusedly both wickedness and goodness dwell,
And hence one might compare thee unto
sparkling wine.

Thy look containeth both the dawn and sunset stars,
Thy perfumes, as upon a sultry night exhale,
Thy kiss a philter, and thy mouth a Grecian vase,
That renders heroes cowardly and infants hale.

. . .

What matter, if thou comest from the Heavens or Hell,
O Beauty, frightful ghoul, ingenuous and obscure!
So long thine eyes, thy smile, to me the way can tell
Towards that Infinite I love, but never saw.

From God or Satan? Angel, Mermaid, Proserpine?
What matter if thou makest—blithe, voluptuous sprite—
With rhythms, perfumes, visions—O mine only queen!—
The universe less hideous and the hours less trite.

~ *Charles Baudelaire, 'Hymn to Beauty'*
{translation by Cyril Scott}

To repeat the words of the Creed, to perform circumcision,
or to lie prostrate on the ground from dread of kingly
power, can avail nothing in the
sight of God:

Obedience is not in prostration on the earth.
Practise sincerity, for righteousness is not borne
upon the brow.

~ *Akbar, as recorded in Abul Fazl's* Akbarnama
{translation by Elliot and Dowson}

I saw a man prostrating himself in prayer, and exclaimed:
'You lay the burden of your nose upon the ground on the
excuse that it is a requirement of prayer.'

~ *The fifteenth-century Sufi teacher Hakim Jami*
{translation by Idries Shah}

You never enjoy the world aright, till the sea itself floweth
in your veins, till you are clothed with the heavens, and
crowned with the stars: and perceive yourself to be the sole
heir of the whole world, and more than so, because men
are in it who are every one sole heirs as well as you.

~ *from* Centuries *by the English poet and religious leader*
Thomas Traherne

Write it on your heart
that every day is the best day in the year.
He is rich who owns the day, and no one owns the day
who allows it to be invaded with fret and anxiety.
Finish every day and be done with it.
You have done what you could.
Some blunders and absurdities, no doubt crept in.
Forget them as soon as you can, tomorrow is a new day;
begin it well and serenely, with too high a spirit
to be cumbered with your old nonsense.
This new day is too dear,
with its hopes and invitations,
to waste a moment on the yesterdays.
~ *Ralph Waldo Emerson*

There is no duty we so much underrate
as the duty of being happy.
~ *Robert Louis Stevenson*

And the growth of the essentials of Dharma is possible in
many ways. But its root lies in restraint in regard to speech,
which means that there should be no extolment of one's
own sect or disparagement of other sects on inappropriate
occasions and that it should be moderate in every case even
on appropriate occasions. On the contrary, other sects
should be duly honoured in every way on all occasions.

Truly, if a person extols his own sect and disparages other
sects with a view to glorifying his, owing merely to his
attachment to it, he injures his own sect very severely by
acting in that way. Therefore, restraint
in regard to speech is commendable, because people
should learn and respect the fundamentals of one
another's Dharma.

This indeed is the desire of the Beloved of the Gods
[Ashoka] that persons of all sects become well-informed
about the doctrines of different religions and
acquire pure knowledge.

~ from Ashoka's Rock edits 7 and 12
{translation by D.C. Sircar}

A man without love, what is courtesy to him?
A man without love, what is music to him?
~ *Confucius*

Every blade of grass and all insects—even these
are my family.
~ *The Malayalam poet Vallathol Narayana Menon*

Can any burden be too great
for those of fit and stable state?
What destination is too far
for those who enterprising are?
Which country is a foreign land
for those with knowledge? And
who can be the enemy
of those who will speak lovingly?
~ *Anonymous Sanskrit poet in* Subhashitavali, *the fifteenth-century
verse anthology compiled by Vallabhadeva*
{translation by A.N.D. Haksar}

Some lines from **Rudyard Kipling**'s *'If', which I look upon as the essence of the message of the Bhagavad Gita in English:*

If you can keep your head when all about you
Are losing theirs and blaming it on you,
If you can trust yourself when all men doubt you,
But make allowance for their doubting too:
If you can wait and not be tired by waiting,
Or, being lied about, don't deal in lies,
Or being hated don't give way to hating,
And yet don't look too good, nor talk too wise;

If you can dream—and not make dreams your master;
If you can think—and not make thoughts your aim,
If you can meet with Triumph and Disaster
And treat those two impostors just the same;

If you can bear to hear the truth you've spoken
Twisted by knaves to make a trap for fools,
Or watch the things you gave your life to, broken,
And stoop and build 'em up with worn-out tools . . .

If neither foes nor loving friends can hurt you,
If all men count with you, but none too much:
If you can fill the unforgiving minute
With sixty seconds' worth of distance run,
Yours is the Earth and everything that's in it [.]

You ask me for the signs of a man of faith?
When death comes to him, he has a smile on his lips.
~ *Muhammad Iqbal*

Is it so small a thing
To have enjoyed the sun
To have lived light in the spring
To have loved, to have thought, to have done?
~ *Matthew Arnold*

The true mystery of the world is the visible,
not the invisible.
We are all in the gutter, but some of us are looking
at the stars.
~ *Oscar Wilde*

I should only believe in a God that would know
how to dance.
~ *Friedrich Nietzsche*

It appears to me impossible that I should cease to exist,
or that this active, restless spirit, equally alive to joy and
sorrow, should be only organized dust—ready to fly abroad
the moment the spring snaps, or the spark goes out,
which kept it together. Surely something resides
in this heart that is not perishable—and life is more
than a dream.

~ *Mary Wollstonecraft*

The mind is its own place, and in itself
Can make a heaven of Hell, a hell of Heaven.

~ *John Milton*, Paradise Lost

What is life if, full of care,
We have no time to stand and stare?

~ *William Henry Davies*

Wisdom begins in wonder.

~ *Socrates*

We have been looking for the burning bush, the parting of
the sea, the bellowing voice from heaven. Instead we
should be looking at the ordinary day-by-day events in our
lives for evidence of the miraculous.

~ M. Scott Peck

A noiseless, patient spider,
I mark'd, where, on a little promontory, it stood, isolated;
Mark'd how, to explore the vacant, vast surrounding,
It launch'd forth filament, filament, filament, out of itself;
Ever unreeling them—ever tirelessly speeding them.

And you, O my Soul, where you stand,
Surrounded, surrounded, in measureless oceans of space,
Ceaselessly musing, venturing, throwing—seeking the
spheres, to connect them;
Till the bridge you will need, be form'd—
till the ductile anchor hold;
Till the gossamer thread you fling, catch somewhere,
O my Soul.

~ Walt Whitman

A good substitute for God is Nature. To respect and delight in the
natural world is to respect and delight in life:

Flower in the crannied wall, I pluck you out of the
crannies, I hold you here, root and all, in my hand, Little
flower–but if I could understand what you are, root and
all, and all in all, I should know what God and man is.

~ *Alfred Lord Tennyson*

I believe in God, only I spell it Nature.

~ *Frank Lloyd Wright*

To see a World in a grain of sand
And a Heaven in a wild flower
Hold Infinity in the palm of your hand
And Eternity in an hour.

~ *William Blake*

The sun, with all those planets revolving around it and
dependent on it, can still ripen a bunch of grapes as if it
had nothing else in the universe to do.

~ *Galileo Galilei*

Listen to the sacred message of Dawn!
Behold the day!
For this is Life, the Soul of Life.
In this brief, swift day is everything,
All the truth of our existence:
The blessing of growth
The rewards of action
The splendour of beauty.
Yesterday is but a dream,
And a dream, too, tomorrow;
Today, well lived, makes
All our days past happy dreams
And our days to come visions of hope.
Welcome, then, this day—
This is the sacred message of Dawn.

~ Kalidasa
{adapted from a translation by A.W. Ryder}

Look at the Sun,
See the Moon and Stars,
Take in the green beauty of the Earth now.
Think.

*~ Hildegard of Bingen, the twelfth-century German nun and musician
(who could also perhaps qualify as a saint, but to me she is more
interesting as a philosopher and composer).*

I believe a leaf of grass is no less than the journey-work
of the stars.

~ *Walt Whitman*

Pass then through this little space of time conformably to
nature, and end your journey in content, just as an olive
falls off when it is ripe, blessing nature who produced it,
and thanking the tree on which it grew . . .

Everything harmonizes with me, which is harmonious to
Thee, O Universe. Nothing for me is too early or too late,
which is in due time for Thee. Everything is fruit to me
which Thy seasons bring, O Nature; from Thee are all
things, in Thee are all things,
to Thee all things return.

~ *Marcus Aurelius*

I feel an indescribable ecstasy and delirium in melting,
as it were, into the system of beings, in identifying myself
with the whole of nature.

~ *Jean-Jacques Rousseau*

There is a pleasure in the pathless woods,
There is a rapture on the lonely shore,
There is society where none intrudes,
By the deep Sea, and music in its roar:
I love not Man the less, but Nature more,
From these our interviews, in which I steal
From all I may be, or have been before,
To mingle with the Universe, and feel
What I can ne'er express, yet cannot all conceal.
~ *Lord Byron, 'Childe Harold's Pilgrimage'*

I have felt
A presence that disturbs me with the joy
Of elevated thoughts; a sense sublime
Of something far more deeply interfused,
Whose dwelling is the light of setting suns,
And the round ocean and the living air,
And the blue sky, and in the mind of man.
~ *William Wordsworth, 'Norton'*

Oh, give us pleasure in the orchard white,
Like nothing else by day, like ghosts by night;
And make us happy in the happy bees,
The swarm dilating round the perfect trees.

And make us happy in the darting bird
That suddenly above the bees is heard,
The meteor that thrusts in with needle bill,
And off a blossom in mid air stands still.

~ *Robert Frost, 'A Prayer in Spring'*

The pride of the peacock is the glory of God
The lust of the goat is the bounty of God
The wrath of the lion is the wisdom of God
The nakedness of woman is the work of God.

~ *William Blake*

The heart of Nature soothes the heart of man,
If with his heart he looks into her eyes.
A place of leaves, wide air, and sunny skies,
Will soothe him more than even woman can.

~ *British poet William Wilsey Martin*

Pied Beauty

Glory be to God for dappled things—
For skies of couple-colour as a brinded cow;
For rose-moles all in stipple upon trout that swim;
Fresh-firecoal chestnut-falls; finches' wings;
Landscape plotted and pieced—fold, fallow, and plough;
And all trades, their gear and tackle and trim.

All things counter, original, spare, strange;
Whatever is fickle, freckled (who knows how?)
With swift, slow; sweet, sour; adazzle, dim;
He fathers-forth whose beauty is past change:
Praise him.

~ *Gerard Manley Hopkins*

Gi[v]e me a spark o' Nature's fire,
That's a' the learning I desire.

~ *Robert Burns*

Give Me the Splendid Silent Sun

Give me the splendid silent sun, with all his
beams full-dazzling;
Give me juicy autumnal fruit, ripe and red from the orchard;
Give me a field where the unmow'd grass grows;
Give me an arbor, give me the trellis'd grape;
Give me fresh corn and wheat—give me serene-moving
animals, teaching content;
Give me nights perfectly quiet, as on high plateaus west of
the Mississippi, and I looking up at the stars;
Give me odorous at sunrise a garden of beautiful flowers,
where I can walk undisturb'd;
Give me for marriage a sweet-breath'd woman,
of whom I should never tire;
Give me a perfect child—give me, away, aside from the
noise of the world, a rural, domestic life;
Give me to warble spontaneous songs, reliev'd,
recluse by myself, for my own ears only;
Give me solitude—give me Nature—give me again,
O Nature, your primal sanities!

~ *Walt Whitman*

I conclude the sequence of hymns and salutations to nature with short poems by two Chinese poets, translated by a man I consider a writer of genius:

In Answer to Vice-Magistrate Zhang

Late in my life I only care for quiet.
A million pressing tasks, I let them go.
I look at myself; I have no long range plans.
To go back to the forest is all I know.
Pine breeze: I ease my belt. Hill moon: I strum
My lute. You ask—but I can say no more
About success or failure than the song
The fisherman sings, which comes to the deep shore.

~ *Wang Wei*
{translation by Vikram Seth}

Question and Answer in the Mountains

They ask me why I live in the green mountains.
I smile and don't reply; my heart's at ease.
Peach blossoms flow downstream, leaving no trace—
And there are other earths and skies than these.

~ *Li Bai*
{translation by Vikram Seth}

Sometimes, prayer can transform people, wiping out all trace of ego and malice, even if momentarily. This is the reason why, even as a non-believer, I am fascinated by the intense lover-like devotion of the Bhakti, Sufi and Christian mystics, and of the poets who follow in their tradition. The best of these poets have produced verse that lives on in songs and poetry collections to this day. The next few pages carry a selection of such verse, beginning with this 'lament' by the English poet **George Herbert**:

Bitter-Sweet

Ah my dear angry Lord,
Since thou dost love, yet strike;
Cast down, yet help afford;
Sure I will do the like.

I will complain, yet praise;
I will bewail, approve;
And all my sour-sweet days
I will lament and love.

He holds me and gently pulls me up
He wipes away the tears I have been crying
He combs my hair and braids them with flowers
He adorns me with ornaments of his choice
He marks my virgin's forehead with vermillion
He puts kajal in my eyes red with weeping.
Then He asks me the reason for my grieving
As He rubs the paste of sandalwood on my breasts

. . .

And I am fooled again by my faithless Lord
I forget my grouse and cover him with kisses.
Sated with His love I sleep and wake
To find Him gone to the other's bed-chamber.

Find Him, friend, look for Tarigonda's Lord
Go, friend, now find and bring him back to me.

~ from 'Vishnuparijatumu', a love song to Vishnu by the Telugu
poetess Tarigonda Venkamamba
{translation by Suhasini}

Batter my heart, three-person'd God; for you
As yet but knock; breathe, shine, and seek to mend;
That I may rise, and stand, o'erthrow me, and bend
Your force, to break, blow, burn, and make me new.
    I, like an usurp'd town, to another due,
    Labour to admit you, but O, to no end.
Reason, your viceroy in me, me should defend,
    But is captived, and proves weak or untrue.
Yet dearly I love you, and would be loved fain,
    But am betroth'd unto your enemy;
Divorce me, untie, or break that knot again,
    Take me to you, imprison me, for I,
Except you enthrall me, never shall be free,
    Nor ever chaste, except you ravish me.

    ~ *from John Donne's 'Holy Sonnets'*

I am He whom I love,
and He whom I love is I:
We are two spirits
dwelling in one body.
If you see me,
you see Him,
And if you see Him,
you see us both.

~ *Mansur al-Hallaj*

*Among the famous Sufis of Punjab is Shah Hussain, the sixteenth-century mystic and poet. He is better known as Madho Lal Hussain, the composite name assumed by him and his lover Madho Lal, a Brahmin boy of Lahore. Here are two of **Madho Lal Hussain**'s kafis, translated by R. J. Yadav, where the love-legend of Heer-Ranjha is used to express spiritual yearning:*

I long to go to my Ranjha's hut—will no one come with me?
I'm down on my knees, I beg and plead,
but I know I must travel alone.
The night is dark, the river deep, the rotting bridge
sways and creaks,
But for this body wounded by desire,
only Ranjha has the cure.

Says Hussain, God's fakir, who but He will comfort me?

Without the Beloved my nights grow longer.
My flesh has fallen away, I'm a bag of rattling bones.
Love won't be concealed when longing's
pitched its camp;
Ranjha's a jogi, now I'm a wanderer—what's
He done to me?

Says Hussain, God's fakir, I hold fast to Your sleeve.

My life is like a broken bowl,
A broken bowl that cannot hold
One drop of water for my soul
Or cordial in the searching cold;
Cast in the fire the perish'd thing;
Melt and remould it, till it be
A royal cup for Him, my King:
O Jesus, drink of me.

~ *Christina Rossetti, 'A Better Resurrection'*

I'm a kafir. A pagan, I worship Love,
I have no need of Islam.
Kafir's wear the thread of their faith,
I have no need of that, either.

I'm drunk on the nectar of His Love. He sings
In my blood: each vein is a thread of my faith.

~ *Amir Khusro*
{translation by R.J. Yadav}

Ramprasad Sen, *a medieval Bengali poet, was a great devotee of Goddess Kali. His unconventional hymns to Kali, like this one, are still sung in Bengal:*

> Enough, Mother, now I'll eat you up.
> A child born in the hour of the evil planet devours
> his mother,
> That's what they say. So devour me first, Mother,
> It's either You or me, there can be no other way.
>
> . . .
>
> I'll eat You up whole, Mother, or die.

> You come to me as early morning's meal each daybreak.
> Your flesh and blood become food and drink for me
> And something wonderful happens.
> Your body mysteriously permeates mine
> And your soul unites with mine:
> I am no longer what once I was.
> ~ *Edith Stein, 'I Will Remain with You . . .'*

In the months of May and June,
In the summer's heat, on a hot afternoon,
Like a fluff of thistledown floating in the air
Casting its shadow on a piece of straw
For a fleeting moment; so hath
Thy love been to me.

Beloved mine! Thy face is like the moon
New risen in the hours of early dawn.
I have treasured the memory of Thy love.
As a traveller numb and cold
Seeks shelter in the wayside hut, and
When rain and sleet beat upon its thatched roof
He lights a fire, guards the glowing embers
In his embrace and lets the dirty water
Leaking through the roof drip upon his back,
So have I cherished Thy love.

~ *Punjabi poet Tara Singh Kamil*

'Twas my one Glory—
Let it be
Remembered
I was owned of Thee.

~ *Emily Dickinson*

I'm restless with the pain of Love—
Who do I tell?
I'm sick with the ache of separation—
Who do I tell?
When was the last time You asked:
Tell me, are you well?

I have no peace at day, nor comfort at night—
Who do I tell?
Some days I think I should send You a message,
But I find no messenger—
Who do I tell?
You stole my heart and thought nothing of it,
You left a wilderness inside—
Who do I tell?

Khusro yearns only for You, none other,
Your beauty is all he desires—
So, who do I tell?

~ *Amir Khusro*

And sometimes the devotee will protest:

> Throw away thy rod,
> Throw away thy wrath:
> O my God,
> Take the gentle path.
>
> For my heart's desire
> Unto Thine is bent:
> I aspire
> To a full consent.
>
> . . .
>
> Though I fail, I weep:
> Though I halt in pace,
> Yet I creep
> To the throne of grace.
>
> Then let wrath remove;
> Love will do the deed:
> For with love
> Stonie hearts will bleed.
>
> ~ *George Herbert, 'Discipline'*

The great Urdu poet **Mirza Ghalib** *on God, sin and Paradise:*

> I fear the secret of the Beloved
> May become known: but for that, there's
> No mystery in dying.

> Why should man feel ashamed of sin?
> What is God's forgiveness for?
> When God is great to grant
> man pardon for his sins,
> when He is indulgent
> to allow him transgression,
> it bespeaks his lack of faith
> to feel ashamed and sad
> and stint his transgressions.
>
> {translation by J.L. Kaul}

> We all know the truth about Paradise, I fear
> But, Ghalib, the illusion keeps the heart in good cheer.

Those who cannot feel the littleness of great things in themselves are apt to overlook the greatness of little things in others.

~ *Kazuko Okakura, author of the Japanese classic*
The Book of Tea

The firm, the enduring, the simple, and the modest are near to virtue.

~ *Confucius*

To love truth for truth's sake is the principal part of human perfection in this world, and the seed-plot of all other virtues.

~ *John Locke*

Not all lamps are lamps; the lamp of truth is the lamp of the wise.

~ *Thiruvalluvar, author of the Thirukkural*

Always tell the truth; then you don't have to remember anything.

~ *Mark Twain*

I like the religion that teaches liberty,
equality and fraternity.
~ *Bhimrao Ambedkar*

We have to learn yet that all religions, under whatever
name they may be called, either Hindu, Buddhist,
Mohammedan or Christian, have the same God, and he
who derides any one of them derides his own God.
~ *Vivekananda*

All besides you are infidels; in the end what does it say?
It makes lunatics of men, what kind of religion is this,
I pray?
~ *Mirza Wajid Husain Changezi*

Do not boast that you have no pride, because it is less
visible than an ant's foot on a black stone in a dark night.
And do not think that bringing it out from within
is easy, for it is easier to extract a mountain
from the earth with a needle.

~ *Hakim Jami*
{translation by Idries Shah}

There is a great spectacle, and that is the sea.
There is a greater spectacle than the sea, and that is the sky.
There is yet a greater spectacle than the sky,
and that is the interior of the soul.

~ *Victor Hugo*

Come you lost Atoms to your Centre draw,
And *be* the Eternal Mirror that you saw:
Rays that have wander'd into darkness wide
Return and back into your Sun subside.

~ *from* Conference of Birds *by Farid ud-Din Attar,*
{translation by Edward Fitzgerald}

When the seeker [and student] by virtue of his *samadhi*
(mental equilibrium) attains an immediate insight into the
nature of the universe, he will recognize that the essence of
all Tathagatas [the Enlightened Ones] and all beings is one
and the same. This is the *samadhi* of oneness.

~ *The ancient Buddhist philosopher Ashvaghosha*

What pang in this lone vigil lies?
Are not the stars your brethren? See;
That silent heaven in majesty,
Drowsed earth, that wilderness, those hills—
Creation one white rosebed fills.
Sweet are the teardrops that have pearled
Like gleaming gems, like stars, your eyes;
What thing is it you crave? All Nature,
Oh my heart, is your fellow-creature.

~ *Muhammad Iqbal*
{translation by V.G. Kiernan}

Let us form one society, one vast family; and since
mankind are all constituted alike, let there henceforth exist
but one law, that of nature; one code, that of reason;
one throne, that of justice;
one altar, that of union.

~ *French philosopher Constantin François de Volney*

Do not do to others as you would not wish done to yourself.

~ *Confucius*

I am certain of nothing but the holiness of the heart's
affections and the truth of the imagination. What the
imagination seizes as beauty must be truth.

~ *John Keats*

Beauty is truth's smile
when she beholds her own face in a perfect mirror.

~ *Rabindranath Tagore*

'Beauty is truth, truth beauty'—that is all
Ye know on earth, and all ye need to know.

~ *John Keats*

Beauty is eternity gazing at itself in a mirror.
But you are eternity and you are the mirror.

~ *Khalil Gibran*

Like Hafiz, drain the goblet cheerfully
While minstrels touch the lute and sweetly sing,
For all that makes thy heart rejoice in thee
Hangs of Life's single, slender, silken string.
~ *Hafiz*
{translation by Gertrude Bell}

Begin at once to live, and count each separate day
as a separate life.
~ *Seneca*

Teach us, Love, above all things, fidelity to music,
Sharpen our responses to the colours of creation,
Lead us undeceptively to what comes after passion,
And let us die, Love, as though we chose to, for a reason.
~ *Nissim Ezekiel*

The passing moment is all that we can be sure of; it is only
common sense to extract its utmost value from it.
~ *W. Somerset Maugham*

God, give us grace to accept with serenity
the things that cannot be changed,
courage to change the things
which should be changed,
and the wisdom to distinguish
the one from the other.

~ from 'The Serenity Prayer' by Reinhold Niebuhr

Ask not—we cannot know—what end
the gods have set for you, for me;
[. . .] How much
better to endure whatever comes,
whether Jupiter grants us additional
winters or whether this is our last,
which now wears out the Tuscan Sea
upon the barrier of the cliffs! Be
wise, strain the wine; and since life
is brief, prune back far-reaching
hopes! Even while we speak,
envious time has passed: pluck the
day, putting as little trust as possible in tomorrow!

~ Horace

Man talks to God in **Muhammad Iqbal**'s *'Khuda aur Banda':*

You made the night, I lit the lamp in it
You made the clay, I moulded it into a goblet.
In the wild wastes, mountains and forests that you made
Orchards, flower beds and gardens have I laid.
It is I who ground stones and turned them into mirrors,
It is I who out of poison extracted its antidote.

I shall gather myself into myself again,
I shall take my scattered selves and make them one,
I shall fuse them into a polished crystal ball
Where I can see the moon and the flashing sun.
~ *from 'The Crystal Gazer' by the American poet Sara Teasdale*

It may be that our role on this planet is not to worship
God, but to create him.
~ *Arthur C. Clarke*

The foregoing generations beheld God and nature face to
face; we, through their eyes. Why should not we also enjoy
an original relation to the universe? Why should not we
have a poetry and philosophy of insight and not of
tradition, and a religion by revelation to us,
and not the history of theirs?
~ *Ralph Waldo Emerson*

In religion and politics people's beliefs and convictions are
in almost every case gotten at second-hand, and without
examination, from authorities who have not themselves
examined the questions at issue but have taken them at
second-hand from other non-examiners, whose opinions
about them were not worth a brass farthing.
~ *Mark Twain*

A people and their religion must be judged by social
standards based on social ethics. No other standard would
have any meaning if religion is held to be necessary for the
well-being of the people . . . Religion must mainly be a
matter of principles only. It cannot be a matter of rules.
The moment it degenerates into rules, it ceases to be
a religion, as it kills responsibility which is an essence
of the true religious act.
~ *Bhimrao Ambedkar*

Excerpts from **Abraham Lincoln**'s *letter to his son's teacher:*

Teach him, if you can,
the wonder of books . . .

[A]lso give him quiet time
to ponder the eternal mystery of birds in the sky,
bees in the sun,
and the flowers on a green hillside.

Teach him to be gentle
with gentle people,
and tough with the tough.

Teach him, if you can,
how to laugh when he is sad . . .
Teach him there is no shame in tears.

Teach him to close his ears
to a howling mob
and to stand and fight
if he thinks he's right.

God reigns when we take a liberal view,
when a liberal view is presented to us.
~ *Henry David Thoreau*

Live a good life.
If there are gods and they are just, then they will not care
how devout you have been, but will welcome you based on
the virtues you have lived by.
If there are gods, but unjust,
then you should not want to worship them.
If there are no gods, then you will be gone, but will have
lived a noble life that will live on in the memories
of your loved ones.
~ *Marcus Aurelius*

We can do noble acts without ruling the earth and sea.
~ *Aristotle*

Father in Heaven who lovest all,
Oh, help Thy children when they call;
That they may build from age to age
An undefiled heritage.

. . .

Teach us the Strength that cannot seek,
By deed or thought, to hurt the weak;
That, under Thee, we may possess
Man's strength to comfort man's distress.

Teach us Delight in simple things,
And Mirth that has no bitter springs;
Forgiveness free of evil done,
And Love to all men 'neath the sun!

~ *Rudyard Kipling, 'The Children's Song'*

Religion is essentially an initiation into inwardness,
a cleaning of internal life. When once the individual
becomes inwardly single, he lives for humanity. He stands
out for truth and fears none even when isolated and
subdued. You may deride him, persecute him,
but he will not retaliate.

~ *Sarvepalli Radhakrishnan*

All human beings are limbs of each other,
having been created of one essence.
When time affects a limb with pain,
The other limbs cannot at rest remain.
If thou feel not other's misery,
A human being is no name for thee.

~ *Sa'adi*

There is no religion without love, and people may talk as
much as they like about their religion, but if it does not
teach them to be good and kind to person and beast,
it is all a sham.

~ *Anna Sewell*

So many gods, so many creeds;
So many paths that wind and wind,
While just the art of being kind
Is all the sad world needs.

~ *Ella Wheeler Wilcox*

Only connect.

~ E.M. *Forster*

Go, little prayer, and wish to all
Flowers in the garden, meat in the hall,
A bin of wine, a spice of wit,
A house with lawns enclosing it,
A living river by the door,
A nightingale in the sycamore!

~ *Robert Louis Stevenson*

ONE

LAST

MISCELLANY

.....

The best lessons for life come from people who work hard, act with integrity and do good without fear of God and Judgement Day. They are usually agnostics—or, at least, 'doubters'—with better morals and greater compassion than many believers. Half of this section is a tribute to such people. The other half is a tribute to mavericks and dissenters. They can sometimes come up with startlingly wise observations. Perhaps because they are eccentric and do not bother with convention, they see aspects of the world that the rest of us are too timid to notice or acknowledge.

Since I am not a very worthy person, and like to broadcast my views and hear people tell me how intelligent and witty I am, I have also put myself in this section. Besides, as an old dissenter, this is where I feel most comfortable.

Indians today are among the most religious-minded people in the world, obsessed with their gods and rituals. But Hinduism did, in fact, accommodate nastika, or atheistic, thought. An ancient school of Hindu philosophy was Charavak. The Charavaks did not believe in God, the Vedas, prayer, sacrifice and other religious rites. They also rejected concepts like the immortal soul, reincarnation, heaven and hell and doing good deeds to earn merit. They were materialists, and valued truth and intellectual rigour. The founder of the Charavak school is believed to have been **Brihaspati**. Almost none of his writings survive. Here is one fragment (translation by M. Rangacharya):

Chastity and other such ordinances are laid down by clever weaklings. Gifts of gold and land, the pleasure of invitations to dinner, are devised by indigent people with stomachs lean with hunger. The building of temples, tanks, wells, resting places, and the like, please only travellers, not others. The Agnihotra ritual, the three Vedas, the triple staff, the ash-smearing, are all ways of gaining a livelihood for those who are lacking in intellect and energy. The wise should enjoy the pleasures of this world through the more appropriate available means of agriculture, tending cattle, trade, political administration, etc.

Is God willing to prevent evil, but not able?
Then he is not omnipotent.
Is he able, but not willing?
Then he is malevolent.
Is he both able and willing?
Then whence cometh evil?
Is he neither able nor willing?
Then why call him God?

~ *Epicurus*

[They say] 'We do not know how this is, but we know that
God can do it.' You poor fools! God can make a cow out
of a tree, but has He ever done so?
Therefore show some reason why a thing is so,
or cease to hold that it is so.

~ *William of Conches, a twelfth-century French philosopher*

If God has spoken, why is the universe not convinced?

~ *Percy Bysshe Shelley*

There can be but little liberty on earth
while men worship a tyrant in heaven.
~ *Robert G. Ingersoll*

Who is he that shall control me? Why may not I act and
speak and write and think with entire freedom? What am I
to the universe, or, the universe, what is it to me? Who
hath forged the chains of wrong and right, of Opinion and
Custom? And must I wear them?
~ *Ralph Waldo Emerson*

Remember: the search for God is not spirituality. In the
ancient yoga sutras God is not discussed, not even
mentioned; there was no need. Later, even when the sutras
mentioned God, they called God a means in the journey of
spirituality and not a goal. It is said that God is useful in
the spiritual practice, in the spiritual search, hence it is
good to accept it; but it is only a means, a device, that's all.
~ *Osho (formerly Acharya Rajneesh)*

Whenever morality is based on theology, whenever the right is made dependent on divine authority, the most immoral, unjust, infamous things can be justified and established . . . Morality is then surrendered to the groundless arbitrariness of religion.

~ *Ludwig Andreas Von Feuerbach,*
the famous German philosopher of the nineteenth century

There is only one step from fanaticism to barbarism.

~ *Denis Diderot, a French philosopher of the Enlightenment*

Guilt is never a rational thing; it distorts all the faculties of the human mind, it perverts them, it leaves a man no longer in the free use of his reason, it puts him into confusion.

~ *Edmund Burke*

To rule by fettering the mind through fear of punishment in another world, is just as base as to use force.

~ *Hypatia, a Greek philosopher and mathematician of Roman Egypt.*
She was accused of witchcraft and 'godlessness' and murdered by a
mob led by an orthodox Christian group.

If a man, holding a belief which he was taught in
childhood or persuaded of afterwards, keeps down and
pushes away any doubts which arise about it in his mind,
purposely avoids the reading of books and the company
of men that call into question or discuss it, and regards
as impious those questions which cannot easily be
asked without disturbing it—the life of that man is
one long sin against mankind.

~ William K. Clifford

The greatest tragedy in mankind's entire history may be the
hijacking of morality by religion.

~ Arthur C. Clarke

Objection, evasion, joyous distrust and love of irony are
signs of health; everything absolute belongs to pathology.

~ Friedrich Nietzsche

If you would be a real seeker after truth, it is necessary
that at least once in your life you doubt,
as far as possible, all things.

~ Epicurus

Fear is the main source of superstition [and]
the parent of cruelty . . . To conquer fear is
the beginning of wisdom.

~ Bertrand Russell

He who will not reason is a bigot; he who cannot is a fool;
and he who dares not is a slave.

~ William Drummond

'In God We Trust.' I don't believe it would sound any
better if it were true.

~ Mark Twain

It is the test of a good religion whether you
can joke about it.

~ G.K. Chesterton

Believing that the Veda are perfect and holy,
Believing in a Creator of the universe,
Bathing in holy waters to gain merit,
Having pride about one's caste,
Performing penance to absolve sins:
These are five symptoms of having lost one's sanity.

~ *Dharmakirti, seventh-century Indian Buddhist philosopher*

God is the greatest calamity.
Yes, people should be godly—that means they should be
truthful, they should be sincere, they should be loving, they
should be conscious. That makes them godly, but that does
not make them God. I am destroying God and spreading
godliness to every human being. It is better that it is spread
far and wide as a quality, as a fragrance, rather than being
confined to a statue in a temple and worshipped.
When you can be it, why worship it?

~ *Osho*

Drukpa Kunley, *also known as Kunga Legpa and The Divine Madman, was not, strictly speaking, an unbeliever (though as a Buddhist he would qualify as an atheist). Yet, I have included him in this section for his 'crazy wisdom'. Because he was a mystic, still greatly revered in Bhutan (where his symbol is an erect phallus), he also appears in the 'Prophets, Mystics and Saints' section of this book. Here, I have included just one of his many startling invocations (translation by Keith Dowman and Sonam Paljor):*

> In this Religious Centre of Holy Lhasa
> Incense and butter lamps are the customary offerings
> To our Only Mother, the Glorious Goddess;
> But today, Duty-Free Kunga Legpa
> Offers his penis and turquoise.
> Accept it, Goddess, and show us compassion!

> If anything is sacred the human body is sacred.
> ~ *Walt Whitman*

Confusion's my fate ever since I renounced wine;
I'm lost and distracted, unable to work;
The pious repent and vow to abstain;
I, too, vowed to abstain—and now I repent.

~ *Babur*

Eat thou and drink; to-morrow thou shalt die.
Surely the earth, that's wise being very old,
Needs not our help. Then loose me, love, and hold
Thy sultry hair up from my face; that I
May pour for thee this golden wine, brim-high,
Till round the glass thy fingers glow like gold,
We'll drown all hours: thy song,
while hours are toll'd,
Shall leap, as fountains veil the changing sky.

~ *Gabriel Rossetti, 'The Choice'*

Do not be too moral. You may cheat yourself out of much
life so. Aim above morality. Be not simply good;
be good for something.
~ *Henry David Thoreau*

I want nothing to do with any order, religious or otherwise,
which does not teach people that they are capable of
becoming happier and more civilized, on this earth,
capable of becoming true master[s] of [their] fate and
captain[s] of [their] soul. To attain this I would put priests
to work, and turn the temples into schools
~ *Jawaharlal Nehru*

Lighthouses are more helpful then churches.
~ *Benjamin Franklin*

Hands that help are far better than lips that pray.
~ *Robert G. Ingersoll*

The belief in a creator is foolish and must be rejected.
If god created the universe,
where was he himself before creation?
If it is said he was transcendent then, existing of himself,
where is he now?
How can an immaterial god create this material world? . . .
If god is perfect, how could the will to create have
arisen in him?
And if he is not perfect, he could no more create the
universe than a potter could.
If he is formless, complete in himself and contains all that is,
How could he have created?
For such a soul would have no desire to create anything.
If it is said that he created to no purpose, on a whim,
then god is pointless.
If he created the world as a sport, it was as the sport of a
stupid child that leads to trouble.
If he created the world out of love for living things,
why did he not make it wholly blissful?
If god were transcendent, he would not create . . .
Uncreated, without beginning and without end,
the world just is,
It endures under the compulsion of its own nature.

~ Mahapurana, *a Jain text composed by*
Acharya Jinasena and his disciple Gunabhadra in the ninth century

I conclude this anthology with some life codes of my own, for every freethinker:

Ahimsa is more than non-violence, it is also the absence of the intention to hurt anyone. It is the first rule of civilization and the central principle of a good life. But it must also be accompanied with a determination to fight bigotry and hate with all one's might.

Religion has very little to do with goodness. Belief in a god does not make a person a better human being, nor does questioning his existence make him an evil one.

Work is worship; worship is not work.

Try not to lie. If you think someone has done you wrong, use truth to bring him around.
Nothing is stronger than the truth.

Anger is a waste of time and energy.
If you cannot forgive, withdraw.

Learn to share what you have. Be generous, and have the
intelligence to know when you are being taken for a ride.

To be happy, rid yourself of greed, envy and hypocrisy.

Connect with nature. Respect it. Find a shady tree and sit
under it for some time every day, watching the life in and
around it. It is better than prayer.

Life is not always fair. Sometimes the good suffer for their
deeds and the wicked prosper. So there is no use telling
anyone that there are rewards for the good in life.
Goodness of the heart should be a habit,
and its own reward.

· *Acknowledgements* ·

My publishers and I gratefully acknowledge the following for permission to use copyright material:

A.N.D. Haksar for his translations of Bhartrihari, Harsha and Vyaasa from *Subhashitavali: An Anthology of Comic, Erotic and Other Verse* (Penguin Books, 2007);

Arvind Krishna Mehrotra for his translations of Kabir's poems from *Songs of Kabir* (Permanent Black-Hachette, 2011);

Javid Chowdhury for Shama Futehally's translation of Meera Bai from *In the Dark of the Heart: Songs of Meera* (HarperCollins, 1994);

Navtej Sarna for a verse from his translation of Guru Gobind Singh's *Zafarnama* (Penguin Books, 2011);

The Estate of A.K. Ramanujan for his translations of Devara Dasimayya and Nammalvar from, respectively, *Speaking of Siva* (reprinted 2007) and *Hymns for the Drowning* (1993);

Ranjit Hoskote for his translations of Lal Ded's vaakhs from *I, Lalla* (Penguin Books, 2011);

Renuka Narayanan for her translation of a verse by Zinda Pil, and translations from the Vedas and the Upanishads, as they appeared in her column 'Faithline' in *The Indian Express* and in *The Book of Prayer* (Penguin Books, 2001);

Rupa Publications for excerpts from Ahmed Ali's translation of Al Quran (2011);

Rupa Publications for Hua-Ching Ni's translations from Lao Tzu's *Tao Teh Ching* (2012) and *Hua Hu Ching* (2012);

Sheikh J. 'Mureed' for his translations of Bulle Shah and Amir Khusro;

Suhasini Nag for her translation of a poem by Tarigonda Venkamamba;

Tulsi Badrinath for Chaturvedi Badrinath's translations from the Mahabharata, as they appear in his book *Mahabharata: An Inquiry in the Human Condition* (Orient Longman, 2006);

Vilas Sarang for his translations of two poems by Janabai;

Vikram Seth for his translations of poems by Wang Wei and Li Bai from *Three Chinese Poets* (Faber & Faber, 1992).

While every effort has been made to obtain permission to reprint copyright material, this has not been possible in a few cases, especially where the original books are out of print. Any omissions brought to our notice will be rectified in future reprints.